T0125391

THE GREAT
WISDOM
GONE BEYOND

First Published by The Buddhist Society 2008
Second edition published by The Buddhist Society 2021

ISBN 978 0 901032 55 3

Printed in the UK

Published by
THE BUDDHIST SOCIETY
58 Eccleston Square
London, SW1V 1PH
T: 020 7834 5858
E: info@thebuddhistsociety.org
www.thebuddhistsociety.org

A catalogue record of this book is available from the British Library

Text, translation and commentary by the Venerable Myokyo-ni

Cover design by Robert & Gail Marcuson
Designed by Avni Patel

In association with
THE ZEN CENTRE
58 Marlborough Place
London, NW8 1PH
E: shoboan_zen_centre@yahoo.co.uk
rinzaizencentre.org.uk

Front cover image by kind permission of The Zen Centre
Title page illustration by kind permission of Vanessa Wan

THE GREAT WISDOM GONE BEYOND

Commentaries on The Heart Sutra and Other Zen Chants

Venerable Myokyo-ni

THE
ZEN
CENTRE

THE BUDDHIST SOCIETY TRUST

CONTENTS

FOREWORD

Acts of devotion play a central role in religion: they help in offering something of myself up to a higher principle. In this way religion is different from other disciplines, such as psychology with which it may overlap from time to time. At the heart of religion is a 'going beyond' this small self or 'I' to recognize and become aware of the presence of something greater of which I am a part.

When turning inward, it is all too easy to become fascinated with my thoughts and feelings. Where I have come from, where should I be going? But this is not going beyond 'I'. Rather, it is putting one head on top of another. This heady 'I' is the basic problem and as the Buddha pointed out in the Four Noble Truths, it is the cause of much of our sorrow. So anything that lifts the heart out of this small self is liberating in the Buddhist sense. This, it is important to understand, is not something that 'I' can do for myself. If I am the problem, then any deliberate act of mine will only increase the sum total of 'I'- consciousness. Thus it is in handing myself over wholly and without any holding back that this liberation can occur. This is the importance of devotional actions.

To begin with, trainees are expected to join in the chanting without necessarily being told what it is they are chanting. This can be a little disconcerting at first. We are not used to it; maybe we are selling our souls without even being aware of it! Usually the resourceful student manages to get a copy of the translations to read, so at least she or he is now aware of the content. However, some of this material is obscure and does not lend itself to immediate understanding. We should remember that apart from Daito Kokushi's admonition, which is in old Japanese, even the monk in Kyoto does not know what he is chanting unless he looks up a translation. After a time, and some study, a degree of intellectual appreciation may arise for the subject matter. But this does not mean that it is now understood in the heart and is seamlessly integrated into life. This can take many years and, doctrinally speaking, lifetimes!

All this may make the trainee wonder what is the point of chanting? But this is precisely the point: there is nothing in it for 'me'. The daily devotional chanting is offered up to the Buddhas and bodhisattvas and for the welfare of all sentient beings. How this chanting will be beneficial is not clear to me, and it does not matter. If I really give my heart to it, each day, with utmost sincerity, then the effect becomes obvious over time. But how it works is a mystery to me, and this is very much the point. The essence of the Buddha's realization he never spoke about. He only showed the way, for the simple reason that it 'passeth beyond human understanding' – it is the very ground upon which we all stand. A mystery is not supposed to be understood; we simply live in its presence and listen to it. That is all.

Venerable Sochu
Shobo-an, June 2008

INTRODUCTION

Religion links us back again to our ground and being. The Buddha, in the Northern persuasion, expounds it as 'All sentient beings are fully endowed with the Tathagata's Wisdom and Power, but sadly, because of their attachments, human beings are not aware of it.' However, an inkling remains, and we somehow long for the sense of awe and wonder which fills the heart and consoles its sorrow.

This longing is particularly strong in times like ours where we have lost not only our religious but also our cultural values. So in our alienated separateness, we cannot help but make pictures to concretize this longing. Again the Buddha, this time in the Southern tradition, 'Now I have seen you, builder of the house. The ridge-pole is broken. Never shall you build new houses again.' The maker of pictures is also the builder of the house. In our 'I' consciousness we see things as distorted by our likes and dislikes, longing and fears. We cannot see them as they really are. Yet, as long as the sense of 'I' is there, which Buddhism sees as delusion, I cannot see 'straight'. I cannot help but see objects according to my Karmic make-up. I see the object, 'I' like or loathe it, etc. And if there is no such painted 'object' – it's not that I then have nothing to like or loathe, etc., for it is not the object that has gone but the one who likes or loathes. This is the Buddha's great teaching of No-I. In this 'I'-less seeing, what Krishnamurti calls 'choiceless awareness', distinctions are clearly seen, tree and house, high and low, but without any additional 'ornamentation', without evaluation or judgement.

Religion, and Buddhism is a religion, leads us back to that clear seeing of what is, the way it really is, which is the Buddha-seeing. It follows that religion is not just a belief in the head but is to be lived. It expresses itself in observances and devotional practices. In that it lightens the strangle-hold of I, thus liberating the human heart that is in all of us and releasing its warmth. This warmth, far greater than an individual heart can contain, then flows naturally forth as wisdom and compassion, touching whatever it comes into contact with.

The chants here discussed are the ones that are chanted in Fairlight and Shobo-an every morning. In between the individual chants, the leader 'turns over' the merit of the chanting.

We do not chant to accumulate personal merit but offer up the merit to the benefit of all. 'May all beings attain Buddhahood.'

Venerable Myokyo-ni

THE REPENTANCE SUTRA

All the evil Karma created by me from of old,
Out of beginningless greed, anger and delusion,
Committed with body, speech and thought,
Of all this I now make full and open repentance.

Comments by Venerable Myokyo-ni

We chant the Repentance Sutra in 'Sino-Japanese' following the Japanese tradition.

Do we ever really consider or spare time to ponder what we chant every day? We can learn so much from it. Terms familiar to us, such as 'repentance', often have different connotations in Buddhism.

'All the evil Karma created by me from of old.' We think we know what 'Karma' means. Do we? We are one-sided and once we have started a Buddhist practice, are more concerned with the practice than the teaching. If we keep the latter in mind at all, it is somehow 'out there', and without noticing we have reverted in our practice to our usual I-orientation with its picking and choosing. Yet it is essential that teachings and practice match, otherwise nothing will change. The Teachings provide the framework against which practice can be matched. That way the Buddhist Teachings take on meaning and substance and so help us to a new way of seeing that leads out of the delusion of I, and hence out of suffering.

'All the evil Karma created by me from of old.' That 'me' is very important. Basic Buddhism teaches the Three Signs of Being: Suffering, Change, and No-I. How then can the Repentance Sutra have anything to do with 'me'? One of the Three Signs of Being is No-I. In the Three Fires ('Out of beginningless greed, anger and delusion'), the delusion is that there is an I. This delusion is then split into greed and anger, liking and loathing. But can a delusion actually produce anything? Can a delusion do anything? Perhaps if we think of delusion simply as I, there is no doubt that I feel liking and I feel loathing and according to that pick and choose. This creates Karma. Karma is the consequence or result of what we usually term 'intentional actions'. Who is the one who intends? Surely 'my' egocentric, opinionated actions. In the Buddhist view, these are not only delusory but also productive of unfavourable Karma. You see how it all comes together. Does that not somehow invite one to go still deeper into the complex of I and its opposite, which is fear?

The Buddhist Teachings help us again if we listen and look carefully. If I hear 'No I', do I really ponder what that No-I actually points to? I have heard many apologies, from Western as well as Eastern teachers, 'Well, it is not really meant like this. It is not completely denied, only certain features of I.' If only certain features of 'I' were denied, we can be quite certain that the Buddhist Teachings would specify them.

Have we ever really looked into what that 'I' is, rather than taking it as absolutely God-given, without which nothing can happen? 'I the doer'. Experiment, experiment! Isn't it that the moment I sit idly, I am feeling rather awkward? Even when sitting Zazen, there is still something I have to do. But say in the dining room, when finished eating and waiting while others are still eating, people start clearing their throats, shuffling and so on. Or, sitting in even our most comfortable chair for a while, can we just relax into it? Or do we reach for the telephone or the radio or the television, pick up a book, or engage in long thought streams? Can we actually peacefully give in to just resting, which we thought we urgently needed because we were tired?

So what is this I, which I believe in but which the Buddha denied? Can we find it? It might seem obvious that it is me. But am I this body? I shall certainly say that I am something different. Then where am I? This is what the Buddha invites us to investigate, to find out about.

For that purpose we need consider the Five Skandhas or Five Aggregates: body, feelings/sensations, perceptions/thoughts, mental formations/reactions (Samskaras, which, when self-centred, are Karma-productive, but not otherwise) and consciousness. We hear such teachings and think, 'Oh yes, the Five Skandhas' and list them automatically. We do not really ponder what they actually mean to us, do we?

As to 'consciousness', we naturally take it as what we normally call consciousness. But it is very clearly stated that each of the Five Aggregates has its own consciousness. There is body consciousness, feeling/sensation consciousness, thought/perception consciousness, mental formations consciousness, and the consciousness of consciousness. That is all that is there. And, says the Buddha, 'In none of these five strands do we find an I'. Yet the bundle functions perfectly. It is I who actually am making mistakes. When acting deliberately, in delusion from of old which taints the Samskaras, such actions are Karma productive. And the Buddha expounds that nowhere in the whole bundle that makes up a human being is an I to be found.

The analogy the Buddha gives is that a cart is certainly a cart. You can ride in it. But then if you begin to take it apart into its components, axle, wheels, carriage body and so on, where then do you find the cart?

So also with the bundle of the Aggregates. There is the body, the most tangible one for us. It had a beginning, has duration and inevitably will also come to an end. In and with that body the other four strands act in harmony; first feeling/ sensation (pleasant or unpleasant), then perceptions/ thoughts generally, then the Samskaras, my likings and dislikings, which have the energy to prompt me to act accordingly, and finally the awareness or consciousness of that action. No I is to be found – or needed! When I hear No-I thus deeply discussed, I do not feel comfortable. A yawning emptiness seems to open, a void that threatens to swallow me. I don't like to think of it, fear it.

What do I think, what do I imagine the state of No-I to be? For a moment let's try. There is no I now. Can we imagine it? The only thing that comes up if we really go into it, is fear of not being. That is where the fear of death comes in, with the fear of loss, of everything that diminishes. That is where the whole 'sea of sorrow' begins and ends. But, actually, when we look, there is no need for I because that bundle works smoothly and much better if there is no I-intentional interference. Only I like and dislike. A cat will find the warmest place in winter quite naturally and if it can't have it, then it goes to the next best place. And in summer it will find the coolest place. That is all there is to it.

And so, what is the use of I? I, the Westerner, say that it is the doer and that without I nothing would be done. But all sentient beings, non-human like the cat, are also doing something, and smoothly within the situation. It is only I who make my life a misery. Where does the I-delusion come from? As we read in the Repentance Sutra, it comes from beginningless delusion spawning desire, greed, fear and anger. I am thirsty. I want to go out. I want the sun to shine. I am not sticking that any longer. I am getting bored. My legs hurt. It is all based on I or on my opinions on how the world should be. And if you agree with me, then it is our opinion of how the world should be. We are against him who has another opinion of how the world should be. It is all I-based.

And if that desire is thwarted I get frightened and angry because then, without the desired cause or object, there seems to be nothing. Really? There is the bundle of the Five Aggregates. What's more, these opinions, wants, convictions, likings, and loathings which I consider to be mine are not 'mine'. They cannot be mine because there is no such thing as an I who can have them. If there were an I and they really were mine, then, if I don't want them, I can lay them down. Try to lay down a good rage. You will find that you cannot do so. Then at the most it can be said that 'I do not have the anger, it has me.' But does it have me? Or is it rather that I am it and it is me and that long habit has convinced us that there is such a thing as I who is angry, because I do not want to be angry. No, I am not angry, I am not nasty. I am calm, I am good, sometimes.

So I distinguish between the changing moods, the good ones I want to keep and the not so good ones I want to get rid of. We all have attempted to do so since childhood and most of us have found that we are not capable of it – we cannot get rid of ourselves. So we have to look at the problem in a different way.

What is that different way? Rather than distinguishing and then choosing 'my' good parts in contrast to those I want to get rid of, just go with the fact that there is anger, there is greed, there are opinions. There are all kinds of things, but they are not 'mine'. The Southern Teachings suggest the formula, 'Not I, not me, not mine'. Whatever comes up, it is 'not I, not me, not mine'. So again back to the Skandhas. There is the body. As long as it is alive, there are all the sensations – hard, soft, painful, pleasant. And there are all the feelings that go with it, equally pleasant or unpleasant or neutral. All these go with the living body.

In the case of a human body, there are also thoughts. Then there are the volitional formations which come from greed and anger, what annoys me, what I find not suitable to me and I dislike. And I like what buoys me up, makes me feel good. 'I' cannot see neutrally. My seeing is coloured by what is experienced as pleasant or unpleasant, as needful or as what has to be got rid of. This is the delusion in which we hang, and the picking and choosing comes from it. So when looking at what is, we cannot see it clearly.

'I like this and dislike that.' I cannot really say why. I try to trump up reasons to 'justify' it. Our life goes like that if we are honest – with one thing and another, all completely arbitrary, as it strikes me, all concerning me, my opinions.

So, in the Five Aggregates there is the body and the four mental strands, and no I can be found. What happens when this body breaks up and is gone, which is what I so much fear?

The mental bundle does not end, has nothing to do with the body. The body is only one of the Five Aggregates. The mental bundle, when it got manifest in that particular body which now has broken up, has had a series of experiences. It might have learned from them or not but whatever, it is no longer the same, has changed during the existence in that body. And now it needs to find, and will find, a form that now 'fits' its present state, which is different from the outlived form.

Its homing into a suitable new form is called rebirth in Buddhism. So rebirth in Buddhism is not a fixed entity that goes through, for this bundle in itself is also ever-changing.

And so we come to Karma. The extent that the body's actions in its life were wilful and self-centred will be appropriately reflected in the bundles' new form and environment. From the Wheel of Change we know the Six Realms of Existence. Latterly this bundle has been in human form in which compassion is also one of the qualities of the heart. Is that not an incentive for doing one's best to ensure good conditions in which the bundle can develop further as it goes into the next form? I think a little less of myself, and thus open up a little more to what is. And then, suddenly I might find that instead of a panic feeling of 'I alone', of losing and dying and then what, there is an emptiness without these mind-produced bogies, an open roominess in which there is a clear continual flowing which has nothing to do with me. This is the Buddha seeing.

Hence the first three lines of the Repentance Sutra, 'All the evil Karma created by me from of old, out of beginningless greed, anger and delusion, committed with body, speech and thought.' Every volitional action – whether by body, in speech or in thought, has its inevitable results. It is obvious though we rarely think about it. It concretely shows whether we are aggressive and rude or fight with each other physically. Speech is a little more subtle. For umpteen reasons, if I-centred, even if I do it 'for your own good', I can be quite hurting with my tongue and can hit under the belt with speech as well as physically. That also needs to be carefully considered so that our language is clear and that we are always aware of what we say. Speaking clearly rather than mumbling anyhow allows consciousness to come in, so that nobody gets hurt or upset, even unawarely.

And then finally there is thought. We tend to continuously mull over our grievances or anger and 'picture' what I should have said and how I would have answered if he or she had said this – long thought streams, all I-centred! In the end, I come out victorious as a fine, upright person having vanquished my enemy. If we habitually indulge in such inner dialogues, we will become more and more irritable. Also, if we do not use the courteous language that befits our time, we become coarser and cruder, for all these things leave their imprint on the bundle of the Aggregates. It is this ever-changing bundle which we need to bear in mind.

When we are told that Daily Life Practice is giving ourselves wholly into what at this moment is being done, does that mean that we should blindly and impulsively give ourselves into whatever is? That is what we mistakenly think, to begin with. But to give oneself into the doing or whatever is at this moment actually means to give oneself over and away. If not given away into the doing, the object orientation with its consequent attachment or aversion arouses energy which now seizes and carries (me) away with inevitable suffering. The Buddha said that because of attachment, we human beings unfortunately suffer and are not aware of the inborn wisdom and power of the Tathagata. We are very rarely clear about the difference between being truly given, being at one with, and being impulsive and/or carried away by attachment. How does that become clear? If I am totally, completely engrossed in gossiping with you, and at that moment someone says something to me, I do not hear him because I am not 'here'. My attention (I) is not here anymore, it is with you over there. Really given into something whole-heartedly, attention is always here, now. This is the living moment.

As when riding a spirited horse, not for a second can one afford to let the attention wander, but that oneness with the horse is at the same time open to see/perceive what is there. You have to be really with it and at the same time wholly in the situation. This being totally with and wholly in the situation is the important thing. Otherwise, we get carried away into blind impulsiveness and are sure to come to grief.

Although we consider ourselves Buddhists and want to do the training, we all too easily forget that the practice is done in ordinary daily life. We rather think that I should not be angry, I should not do this, that or the other, I should be 'cool'. So I deaden myself, I get so 'cool' that nothing will touch me anymore. Then underneath the energy begins to pile up, and for no reason whatsoever, perhaps after years, it suddenly blows, wreaking havoc all around. If you look about it is not uncommon. Who would want to have such a fate?

Better to do what Master Rinzai enjoins, 'Be your natural selves and don't give yourselves any airs.' Instead, work carefully and get clear on the Buddha's Teaching. Seen from its perspective, things look different and somehow much more manageable because they are no longer I-centred.

So that bundle of the Five Aggregates rolls on, ever-changing, with no 'I' to be found. And according to 'my' behaviour, the strands and with them the bundle, will become finer or coarser. According to that, one body gone, a now more fitting form will be found – it need not be human. 'I', when I have a glimpse of emptiness, feel fear. But in Buddhist view, void or emptiness is not empty at all, is just what is, only it has no centre called I anymore. Then, seeing is much clearer and what I was frightened of, including 'my' dying and what will then happen to 'me', is gone. With delusion (I) gone, what is, is there, will always be there and will always continue changing. So the bundle can change with cultivation (practice), depending on actions, speech and thought, effecting a growing understanding. Thus fewer difficulties arise and so things become less and less sorrowful, go smoother and smoother.

All strands of the mental bundle change, go on ever changing. When the form falls off, the rest will transfer into another form that will fit it now.

When I was forty, I had a particular dress which I was very fond of. In time it was worn out. But even if I had it now, I could not wear it, 'my' form, too, has changed completely. The 'mental' bundle, I hope, has also changed from between forty and eighty.

Our outlook is our own 'mental' bundle and it changes. With cultivation, what agitates and frighten us falls away. But we have to be clear about the process, and for this we need the Buddha's Teachings. Usually we are tied into the framework of our I-centred thinking. Just this becomes clear and is experienced in practice when we have the Buddhist framework. It helps us to look at things in a different way and makes us face things which by nature we shy away from. Although the practice is by no means perfect, certain things begin to emerge and are actually born out, and so we have more trust and confidence to continue.

Then we ponder again. And the more we ponder this new framework, the Buddha's Way, which to begin with we did not understand, slowly a few things become quite familiar, as does the new framework. Thus carried by our own continued practice, things will truly change. But if the framework is forgotten or not matched by practice, how can anything change? How can I, who am always the centre, be forgotten? Our very thinking is based on 'I' picking and choosing.

As things get clearer and clearer, awareness and confidence grow. It does go without me after all! As a matter of fact, it goes considerably better without me. Then slowly it becomes possible to give over more and more to that new framework, the new seeing, the new way of thinking, the new way of perceiving – and that is the purpose of the Buddhist training.

So far the first two lines of the Repentance Sutra. Next comes, 'Committed with body, speech and thought, of all this I now make full and open repentance.' I do not like to admit that I have been or have done wrong. I like to make quite sure that if I do something, it will be done right, otherwise I would rather not do it and wait until I know how to do it. But if I for example want to learn to ride a bicycle, and read up about riding bicycles expecting I can then do it, I shall never ride a bicycle.

But there is a time when I have to chance it. In all learning, I have to face the fact of doing wrong. Why can't I bear it? It comes down to the same thing, not being able to do something, or failing, diminishes 'me'. If that is beginning to get clear from what has been said so far, then we take it as natural that as a single individual, I cannot know everything and cannot do everything. There are certain things that I can learn to do and others that I have not much talent for and will never really properly learn. There are things that I can and do know and others that I cannot know and do not know. When I play a game or whatever, sometimes I win and sometimes I lose. Why should that be so very upsetting? Why should I not admit it? Here we are down to the roots of I. But with proper training, it is not such a very great deal anymore because this new, neutral seeing is no longer I-centred. When once more I have made a fool of myself, I can take it, knowing I am capable of failing. Working on it to iron it out, serves to prevent me from repeating the blunder and so becoming less prone to make a fool of myself.

That alone is quite a different outlook. Of all the wrongs that I have committed 'I now make full and open repentance.' Rather than wearing ash and sackcloth, and crying that 'I am the greatest sinner' – which all comes down to I again – just to be honest and open, knowing that we all have failings and weaknesses, etc. and actually share them with each other. In this sharing we find a real community and a communal understanding of each other which releases us from that desperate aloneness from which I, every I, suffer as separate from everything else and from which stems my need to always feel right and good and which, of course, I can never live up to.

But even more, from this repentance, from this seeing and feeling sorry, it also becomes clear that in my foolishness or worse, whatever I have perpetrated, I have hurt others as well as myself. If I feel truly sorry for that rather than wearing ash and sackcloth, it is unlikely I will repeat it again. But also from that arises an understanding of and compassion for each other. Like everything else, compassion starts at home. If we do not have compassion for ourselves and our frequent failings, and rather than hiding them start ever again, there will be no tolerance of others either. At most, we hide our ruthlessness under a sentimental cloak.

Full and open repentance opens out from a narrow, limited I to that full humanity of which the Buddha said that it is endowed with the wisdom and power of the Tathagata, but that because of our attachments we are not aware of it. However, there is an intimation in all of us that there is something lacking, and just this is the source of our basic dissatisfaction, Dukkha, whatever it is pictured as. I need/want something – this is actually an intimation that there is something more than and beyond I, and it will not give me peace. If I take it as an object outside me and run after one of those blind attachments, a new house or a new car or a new religion or whatever it might be, the longing will remain. What it points to is something more and bigger and wider than I. But as long as I picture it as outside and believe I can get it from there, I am still in the duality of I wanting to get something, and this is not possible, because it is inside. As Master Mumon said, 'The treasures of the house do not come in by the front door.' To awaken to that is what the Buddha pointed at, and it is not something that 'I' can 'get'.

Just this is what makes the training so hard and especially for us Westerners so difficult to understand. In short, it is not 'some-thing' at all. Thus it is not something that I can get from outside, not something that I can find inside either, however much I dig, observing myself and my slightest whims. 'I' can be carried away by this, that or the latest of my fancies. None of these will help. There is only that basic delusion of I, and that is also the attachment to I, to a non-existent ghost, and unless that is truly seen into and slowly worn away, it will obscure the view, it will veil the understanding, it will veil the insight. Therefore I cannot cut myself off by an act of will, and even the utmost asceticism will not do so, as the Buddha found out. Or the greatest fooling of myself by trying to cut off the physical senses, to cauterize them. It will not do it.

So insight into what actually is begins to dawn – that things go quite well without me, that they do not need me, and are in any case not under my control and do considerably better without me. Then slowly, slowly, that hard little ball of 'But I ..., but I ... ' begins to shrink, wither away and drop off like a leaf in autumn. 'I' is not something that I can cut, or that anybody can cut; it is not for cutting, because it is not some-'thing'. This is why the practice is long and needs patience, endurance and faith, and needs again and again the pondering of those simple teachings and the framework that Buddhism gives us, so that we may come to the same insight to which the Buddha awoke. When the heavy burden of 'I' has finally dropped off from the shoulders of a body, the 'bundle' is free. Meanwhile, at the demise of a specific body and depending on how it is now, the 'bundle' is attracted to a now suitable form or to no more form. No I can be found, nor is one necessary.

When the 'bundle' is freed from the delusion of 'I' then as a Mahayana saying puts it, 'The heart rolls with the ten thousand things, this rolling is truly mysterious.' We have heard that saying often but perhaps with slowly developing insight it takes on a profound meaning, becomes music and uplifting. There is no one who wants to understand, there is no one who wants to appropriate it, the heart just freely rolls. Master Rinzai likened it to a gourd bobbing on a stream, or a fish playfully leaping in the water. That is the end of I and the end of fear. So when we chant the Repentance Sutra every morning, it opens up to a new perception. The heart widens and releases its warmth and in rolling with the ten thousand things it benefits them all.

We chant the Repentance Sutra to look at all the harmful, hurtful but most of all silly and idiotically stupid things we have perpetrated since beginningless time and thus willy-nilly interfered with, and possibly harmed, others. For that we can and do whole-heartedly feel sorry. This feeling sorry is repentance and it is important because it will restrain us from doing the same again.

Feeling truly sorry is very different from feeling guilty. The latter oppresses, is a burden that stifles. But in feeling truly and deeply sorry, the whole heart can and does turn over. In that 'change of heart' something happens. This does not apply only to Buddhism. In Christianity, we think of it in terms of conversion, like that of Saul to Paul on the road to Damascus.

A classic Buddhist example is Angulimala, who was a murderer. He had collected the fingers of the people he had murdered and strung them into a necklace of 999 such fingers. And he had determined that the thousandth would be that of the Buddha. He sneaked up behind him intent on murdering him and cutting off one of his fingers. The Buddha was well aware of it and just when the stalker had caught up with him with the knife already raised, he quietly turned round and looked at him calmly, neither angry nor defensive. His strength and compassionate radiance was so great that Angulimala suffered a complete change of heart, dropped the knife and fell down at the feet of the Buddha. With his heart completely emptied of all former intents, he asked to be taken on as his disciple.

And so, we first of all chant the Repentance Sutra; and when the heart is truly sorry and ready to turn, we then need something that gives a new purpose, a new value and that helps us in our life. Without that, however sorry we may feel, nothing much will happen. But if we can from out of true repentance look up to something that is more than I, we are ready to begin a training under a teacher who is in accord with the old masters.

GOING FOR REFUGE

I take refuge in the Buddha. I take refuge in the Dharma. I take refuge in the Sangha. I take refuge in the Buddha, the most venerable one. I take refuge in the Dharma, venerable in its purity. I take refuge in the Sangha, venerable in its harmony. I have taken refuge in the Buddha. I have taken refuge in the Dharma. I have taken refuge in the Sangha. I put my faith in the true Tathagata of complete and perfect Enlightenment. He is my great master. I will rely on him as my teacher and not follow evil demons or other ways. Out of compassion, out of compassion, out of great compassion.

Comments by Venerable Myokyo-ni

A training without Refuge or teacher is not likely to carry anywhere because there is nothing to look up to and nobody to guide us and so it very soon comes down again to just my own ideas. So we take Refuge in the Buddha, Refuge in the Dharma and Refuge in the Sangha. The Buddha, a human being like us who, by his own strength, awakened to that genuine insight of seeing all things as they really are, which is the Dharma. The Buddha re-discovered the Dharma in its fullness, and so taking Refuge in the Buddha also means to take Refuge in the Dharma. These two are often put together as 'Refuge in the Buddha-dharma'. It is the Way all things really are, and from that insight the Buddha also taught the way out of suffering, out of our self-inflicted difficulties towards a clear seeing. From that, then, derives a willingness to take our place and to play our part in the scheme of things as it really is.

As the Buddha died long ago and we need to have some assistance in our endeavour, we take refuge in the Sangha, in those who have followed or are following the Buddha's Way.

As we look at the long line of those who have spent their lives following in the Buddha's footsteps, and have arrived at the same seeing and speak as with one voice, we can trust their teachings and their advice. Having thus pondered, 'I again take refuge in the Buddha, the most venerable one.'

It is said that all of us, if we really bestir ourselves sufficiently, will come to genuine insight provided we go through a specific training, listen to the Buddha-dharma and persevere in spite of all difficulties. But to be able to do so, four propitious conditions have to come together: to be born at a time of a Buddha, at a place where the Buddha's teaching is extant, to come into contact with it, and to incline towards it. Surely the fruit of good Karma! So, 'I take Refuge in the Buddha, the most venerable one. I take Refuge in the Dharma, venerable in its purity. I take Refuge in the Sangha, venerable in its harmony'.

Would you like to join a squabbling lot of people, each one with their own opinions and ideas? Or would you rather trust the Buddha? When he expounded his teachings to the Kalamas, they asked, 'Lately, other teachers have also come and talked to us and each one said that he alone had the whole wisdom and truth. We do not know whom we should follow?' The Buddha said, 'Do not believe anyone because you think that he knows. Do not believe anybody who says that he knows. Just yourselves look. Is what has been said in harmony and in line with what has always been said by the wise of all times? If so, and it

makes sense to you, and if your heart inclines to it, then try it.'
But not just for a day – give it a good try. If, following it under
instruction, 'you find that it leads to peace of heart, harmony,
joy and happiness, you will quite naturally continue. But if you
find that it does not lead to peace of heart, harmony and joy,
then throw it away.'

It could not be said clearer. Those who have gone that way
have, as it is recorded in the Scriptures, also spoken with one
voice, assuring us that 'the Dharma is lovely in the beginning,
lovely in its middle and lovely in its consummation.'

Members of the Sangha are not only our preceptors but
also our examples. They live a life that we feel is difficult to
live. So, we take Refuge in the Buddha, in the purity of the
Dharma which is just as it is and in the Sangha in its harmony.
Having considered all that, now again 'I have taken Refuge in
the Buddha. I have taken Refuge in the Dharma. I have taken
Refuge in the Sangha.'

We chant the Refuges after the Repentance Sutra. Both of
them are very short and we chant them three times. They set us
up for the day, emptying the heart of all images which is another
form of meditation. Then there is no need to fret or worry any
more. We have taken Refuge in the Buddha, have taken Refuge
in the Dharma, have taken Refuge in the Sangha. Now we can
move into the day guided and aware, and, hopefully, we shall
not stray too far from the Way.

Next comes, 'I put my faith in the true Tathagata of complete
and perfect Enlightenment.' The 'true Tathagata of complete
and perfect Enlightenment' is not Shakyamuni, who has long
since died. Rather, it is the Buddha-nature which is inborn in
all of us and of which the Buddha himself said that he had only

re-discovered an ancient path leading to an ancient city. It is the inalienable birthright of every human being. We are all endowed with the same insight and the same power that Tathagatas have. Only, the Buddha told us, because of our attachments, sadly we are not aware of it. So we just put our faith in the true Tathagata of complete and perfect Enlightenment. By getting out of the way, we give him room in a heart that has been emptied or 'purified'.

Throughout his Teaching, the Buddha set out the Way, patiently and compassionately, expounded it in parables, taught it in this and that version, but always the same Way. Along this Way he set up signposts that we can follow. He reiterated the same points so as to really impress it on the clods that we are. That 'true Tathagata of complete and perfect Enlightenment' is familiar with our difficulties and our weaknesses and encourages us, saying, 'Look! It is there in you, just get out of the way.' Into him I put my faith, truly.

The Zen School holds that for walking the Way, three things are necessary: a Great Root of Faith, faith not in some kind of abstract statement but in the inherent true Tathagata of complete and perfect Enlightenment. How can I believe it? In our best moments or at moments of extreme danger or sometimes somehow, something struck us out of the blue, something broke through. We remember such moments as great, but we believe it was the occasion rather than the Buddha-nature shining through. We experience it as great, and this is what 'strikes' us, why we remember it. The true Tathagata in the own heart is overlaid and covered by I, but he is there and into him I put my faith.

'He is my great master', his Teachings are my great master. I heed those Teachings and do not offend against them. But when we have been in training for some time, the novelty wears off and we tend to backslide. There is our personal life, possibly family life, there is our professional life, our work, and we also want to have some time for ourselves! Then all too often there is 'no time' for 'my' training. When it comes to a toss-up, is the training really important to us? As in the Buddhist analogy, is it as urgent as if our head were held under water? Would we then think, 'Well, I suppose I'll wait until it's all over.'?

And so, if I really put my faith in it, it is remarkable what in faith becomes possible. There is a saying in Christianity that faith can move mountains. We say, 'Ha, ha. Today we know better.' But what faith can actually do is quite unbelievable. Can you walk on the ridge of a roof? Yet a sleepwalker does it without any difficulty, not being aware of an I that is judging it as dangerous. But if someone yells and wakes him up, he will come to himself, see where he is and fall down. True faith can do the same – 'I' is forgotten, it goes 'beyond I'. Have we ever thought of a sleepwalker as a good example of what strength and possibilities there are in a quite ordinary human body? And so, 'I put my faith in the true Tathagata. He is my great master.'

Faith, if really whole-hearted, is of supreme help. For it, nothing is difficult. This faith, then, is my great master, the Tathagata. If I can put my faith in him, then following his teachings and his footsteps is not difficult. Taking the Three Refuges reminds us of that. And so what I call a difficult day ahead, or problems besetting me, all this begins to lessen if faith is great enough.

From that arises the next resolution, 'I will rely on him as my teacher.' The various schools, southern and northern, tell the Buddha's life story. Although the descriptions differ slightly, the salient points are common to all. They indicate the stages on the Way, are signposts to follow, stages we have to pass.

What does 'leaving home' mean? Leaving our well-established convictions, opinions, habits, and being willing to open up and learn to look anew. In doing so we also find out where the limits of the body's endurance are. This is the austerity phase. Although austerities alone will not produce anything, knowing that the limits are in fact much larger than I thought possible is important for the next stage. There, things that I thought were 'me' begin to fall off. As with the Buddha, born a prince, leaving 'home', refusing to succeed the two greatest teachers, finally disowned by his last five disciples, he had nothing left. When there is nothing more to fall off, then the inner film begins to roll. So Mara appeared, with his daughters and his demons. But, with nothing left, the Three Fires (delusion, lust and fear/aversion) lack fuel and have died down. Where there is nothing, neither lust nor fear can have any inroad.

This is what the 'Tathagata' means, the strength not to be touched by any forces, outer or inner. That is our birthright, the inherent wisdom and power of the Tathagata.

So, 'I rely on him as my teacher and will not follow evil demons or other ways' – will not be tempted by Mara, will not become a Devadatta. Devadatta, the Buddha's cousin, was ambitious and envious of the Buddha. He even tried to kill him but was foiled again and again. 'Not follow ... other ways' – these 'other ways' are non-Buddhist or other ways than the true Dharma. This is particularly important for us now because in our simplistic thinking, we believe that the more we can scratch together from everywhere, the wiser we are. So we indiscriminately read and go here, there and everywhere, try a little of this and a little of that, only to get even more confused than we are anyway. Then we are in real trouble. 'Here they told us to sit looking inwards, there we were sitting facing the wall, here we were told that, there we were told this.' Even traditional lines go different ways, have different stages. The task is difficult enough, no need to add to it. Read the Zen texts. There have always been those who rather than bestirring themselves, just hold on to one aspect at best. 'I know', and write books about it – and their books usually read very well. By indiscriminate reading too, we become even more bewildered or are carried away into intellectual speculations and become critical ourselves, judging – as we see it.

With all this we forget to keep our nose to the grindstone. Cultivating our own practice is all-important. The Three Refuges state it very clearly, 'not follow evil demons or other ways'. If we undertake the training, then we stick to it for at least a reasonable time. If we immediately start running about here, there or anywhere, it does not work. The Dalai Lama on one of his visits suggested, 'Be very choosy before you actually settle under a teacher. Only do so if you feel really and truly that a relationship is possible. But if so, then stick to it!'

The extremely good fortune of this old woman was that, without even knowing it, I was pitched straight into circumstances in which I met Sesso Roshi. I am reasonably convinced, and say with deep gratitude, that if it had not been Sesso Roshi and the trust I had in him, I do not think I could have managed the first few years of the training. So it is sticking it out, having faith and finding one's limits. And 'not to be deceived', as Master Rinzai admonishes.

A 'man of Zen' does not lend himself to any personality cult. 'What a great teacher I have', and a projection line is thrown out but rattle, rattle, it falls down. Another one is projected, 'What a magnificent saying this is', and rattle, rattle, it clangs down again. That is what was learned from the few real Dharma carriers that I have had the great good fortune to meet. One cannot hang a projection on to them, they have no hooks to engage them. And this is, I think, a general gauge. If you throw out a projection and it finds a hook, a little demon feeds from it!

For the need to feed, there is a story about such a little demon. Shaka, the king of gods, was away while all the gods were assembled in his throne room. Suddenly a shabby little demon scampered in, shinned up on Shaka's throne and settled himself on it. The gods began to murmur, 'Look at that shabby little demon who dares to climb up on Shaka's throne. There he sits, giving himself the airs of Shaka. My goodness, he grows, he is beginning to look like him! How can such a terrible thing happen?' All the while, the shabby demon grew and became more and more like Shaka. Then Shaka himself came in. The gods implored him, 'Look what has happened. There he sits. He looks almost like you. He came in, a little shabby demon, climbed up and usurped your seat. Throw him out!' Shaka, very ceremoniously, walked up to his own throne, knelt down on one knee with folded hands and announced, 'I, Shaka, king of the gods, have come to salute you'. When the demon heard that, he shrunk considerably. A second time, 'I, Shaka, king of the gods, salute you', and the demon shrank even further. And when he heard it a third time, 'I, Shaka, king of the gods, salute you', he had become again the shabby little demon, shinned down from the throne and ran away whimpering. In a way it is an amusing story, but it has a lot of punch behind it. Let's remember that.

'I put my faith in the true Tathagata of complete and perfect Enlightenment. He is my great master. I will rely on him as my teacher and not follow evil demons or other ways. Out of compassion, out of compassion, out of great compassion.' Why 'out of compassion'? In order to rely on him and follow him, where does the compassion come in? If there is no realization of the non-existence of I and of everything being interconnected, then warmth of heart is lacking and so is the willingness to play one's part. For this, it is necessary to know what that part is and not to blindly play it but out of the interconnectedness of what wants to be done. That points then to the Four Vows, the first of which is to be of assistance to all sentient beings. This means to be of suitable help to those we are in contact with and of good will to all beings.

There is a passage in the 'Inexhaustible Lamp' by Master Torei which is worthwhile reading and re-reading. He says that compassion is to see that all things can smoothly function in their allotted parts, a knife to cut, feet to walk, a handkerchief to wipe noses and tears, a needle to sew. And to help them so that they can function in their respective roles and not be misused – a knife not to weed with, a pair of scissors not to cut stone with. That is compassion. Not intentionally to go out to find something or somebody that 'I' can now help – that is all I-manifestation. But it is just to be and see what is necessary.

I remember my first few months in Japan. It was the New Year and my Dharma father had taken me to a tea ceremony which was given by one of the big tea houses in Kyoto for the Daitoku-ji priesthood. I came as his disciple, diligently walking after him. My Dharma father, at whose temple I was staying, liked to say that, 'A true man of Zen has the head of a tiger and the legs of a cow!' It could be his photograph. He lived to 105, only a bit deaf and in a wheelchair. He wanted to talk to Sesso Roshi on the way back on that New Year's day. With noticeable impatience, he adjusted his speed to that of Sesso Roshi who was very slow. Now my temple father liked to be up early, sweeping in front of the temple and setting everything to right. On the way out, one of the heavy gates had got unhooked and was swinging dangerously in the high wind. My temple father, intent on talking and impatient, noticed nothing. Without even stopping, slow Sesso Roshi took hold of the huge iron hook, clicked it in and walked on. If I had not been directly behind him, I would not have noticed, so smooth was that action. Later, we saw a street sign blown over and again he righted it in passing – one smooth action. At that moment, I knew that if at all possible, this was going to be my teacher. I knew that my temple father had quite different plans for me and there seemed to be nothing I could do but circumstances arranged themselves so that, after all, I was sent to train under him.

I can only be deeply grateful – not only to Sesso Roshi, the Tathagata in the form of Sesso is what we need to recognize. Such teachers will never try to take us over. They will only point, as the Buddha said to the Brahman, 'Buddhas only point the way.' In that we take refuge, in that we put our faith and our trust. That trust will grow and in a miraculous way we will find again and again that if we just go on with the training, help and support are forthcoming. All we need to do is to bow and do our very best, however poor that may be, and to stick with it.

That is also what the Great Root of Faith means. And that then turns into compassion. This is what the teachers point to, all of them, right from the Buddha – that long line of Patriarchs and of Arhats.

If we are interested only in great things somewhere else and forget to do diligently our own, then we miss that being given over. And so we come back again, as we always do in practice, to the diligent walking of the Buddha's Way, following it with joy and with a confidence which makes the walking rewarding. It does not matter how 'far' we go. There is no exam at the end of the Way. Every step is its own reward because there is no particular 'This is the end. I must be enlightened.' Each and every step is its own reward if walked with faith and goodwill. Then goodwill flows out unhindered, and in that goodwill our surroundings are clearly seen. On a summer evening, if the flowers droop, we just go and water them. We do not need to make a general enquiry or to ring up a garden expert to ask why the plants are wilting. And so we become caring and assist all towards their proper function – and just that is compassion, great compassion. If we have learned giving in to the small things, we suddenly find that in the same way we understand each other, and from that we can give others a helping hand in quite a different way than if I try to do it from my own small littleness. That is why we go for Refuge. And that is why compassion arises of itself.

THE HEART SUTRA

When the Bodhisattva Avalokitesvara practised the profound Great Wisdom Gone Beyond (Prajna Paramita), he clearly saw that the Five Aggregates (Skandhas) are all empty and thus passed beyond suffering. Oh Sariputra, form is not different from emptiness, emptiness is not different from form. Form is emptiness, emptiness is form. The same applies also to feeling/sensation, perception, mental configurations and consciousness. Oh Sariputra, all things (dharmas) are in themselves empty, neither coming to be nor ceasing to be, neither pure nor impure, neither increasing nor decreasing. Thus within emptiness there is no form, no feeling/sensation, no perception, no mental configurations, no consciousness. Within emptiness there is no eye, no ear, no nose, no tongue, no body, no thought; there is no field of seeing, of hearing, of smelling, of tasting, of touching, no field of consciousness. Within emptiness there is no delusion nor extinction of delusion and so on (through the Twelve Links of Arising due to Conditions [Chain of Dependent Origination]) to old age and death, nor extinction of old age and death. Within emptiness there is no suffering, no cause of suffering, no end of suffering and no way to the end of suffering. Within emptiness there is no knowledge, no attainment and nothing that can be attained. The Bodhisattva relies on the Great Wisdom Gone Beyond and so his heart is free of hindrances. Because his heart is free of hindrances, he is free of fear. Going beyond all error and delusion, he enters final Nirvana. All past, present and future Buddhas rely on the Great Wisdom Gone Beyond and so attain to

Perfect and Complete Awakening. Know therefore that the Great Wisdom Gone Beyond is the Great Mantra, the Wisdom Mantra which is supreme and peerless and delivers from all suffering. It is true, not vain; therefore it is proclaimed the Mantra of the Great Wisdom Gone Beyond and is proclaimed thus: GATE GATE PARAGATE PARASAMGATE BODHI SVAHA! (Gone, Gone, Gone Beyond, Gone Altogether Beyond, Enlightenment Fulfilled.)

Comments by Venerable Myokyo-ni

The Heart of the Great Wisdom Gone Beyond Sutra, generally referred to as the Heart Sutra, is the heart or gist of the Mahayana or Great Way school. It arose in India perhaps a couple of centuries after the Buddha's Parinirvana and can be seen as the mother of all the Mahayana teachings. This Great Maha Prajna Paramita teaching, to give it its Sanskrit name, is summarised in the short sutra that we chant every day, the Heart Sutra.

Its very clear message is that since we are all suffering from delusion, just look, just look! There is no self-nature, no I. Not only in me, but in no 'thing' can we find anything that permanently remains the same. Even seas change in time. Even mountains get worn away. There is no permanent entity anywhere to be found. And this is what the Heart Sutra, the gist of all the Paramita texts, tries to make us understand.

When we chant Makka Hannya Haramita Shingyo, 'Makka' is Sanskrit 'Maha', 'Hannya' is 'Prajna', 'Haramita' is 'Paramita' and 'Shingyo' is Heart Sutra. While chanting, we do not much dwell on the meaning, but chant it with a whole and full heart. If we really give ourselves into it, after the chanting our hearts are wide open and empty.

In mediaeval Japan, a monk had to chant the Hannya Shingyo in one breath to prove that he had the extraordinary qualities and strength to be entrusted with founding a temple. Try it! Perhaps this is the reason why in Japan sutras are chanted so fast.

To empty the heart, to purify it, is the purpose of the Buddhist training. If the heart is truly empty, attachments, thoughts, opinions are no longer there. The Buddha said, 'All beings are inherently endowed with the Tathagata's wisdom and power. But sadly human beings, because of their attachments, are not aware of it.' My delusive attachments prevent this awareness and so also the appropriate response. Wisdom then is the insight, the clear seeing of what is, and power is the strength to conform with what is. Without deluded attachments, the wisdom and power of the Tathagata will come into play instead of I bungling or messing about.

Now we can look at what the Heart Sutra says. The Bodhisattva Avalokitesvara practised the profound Great Wisdom Gone Beyond. The Bodhisattva Avalokitesvara is called Kanjizai in the sutra, he who sees and hears everything. In Japanese 'Kanzeon' or 'Kannon' means he 'Sees and Hears'. He is the Bodhisattva of Great Compassion, often paired with Manjusri, the Bodhisattva of Great Wisdom. Avalokitesvara is said to have come to insight through sound. Genuine insight arises when a sense contact reflects in an 'empty heart'. Very rarely, if at all, do we hear of insight arising in meditation.

We have no history about it, but tradition holds that on a clear winter morning the Buddha came out of deep meditation, saw the morning star glittering in the icy cold sky and 'awoke'. When the heart is truly empty with nothing left in it, then what falls into it from outside is reflected directly, and in that the insight becomes conscious. So Avalokitesvara came to his insight by way of sound, and in all Mahayana Schools it is believed that he hears the crying for help and, being a Bodhisattva, will respond and succour.

The Heart Sutra says that the Bodhisattva Avalokitesvara practised the profound Great Wisdom Gone Beyond. And what he saw was that the Five Aggregates are all empty, and at that he passed beyond suffering.

Passing beyond suffering is the aim of the Buddha's Way. The Buddha himself said, 'Suffering I teach and the way out of suffering.' We have to understand that correctly. Suffering is a part of this world in which we live, it is inescapable. We all know it. The Buddha found the way out of suffering and taught it to all those willing to listen. In our more joyful moments, deluded as we are, we believe that there should be no suffering, that it is not right that I suffer and I complain bitterly if I have as much as a headache or a toothache. But in this our world there is suffering, and there is no way of avoiding it. Sooner or later, change, which is also inevitable, takes something I love away and there is pain, and sooner or later there is death. It is a fact of life, as is night and day, and it is not possible to avoid it. Suffering can be pretty gruesome, as we know from those three fateful encounters of the young Prince Gautama. It is very clearly stated, right from the beginning.

Avalokitesvara realized that the Five Aggregates are all empty and thus passed beyond suffering. The bundle of these Five Aggregates (Skandhas) is what makes up a human being. With the individual strands and the bundle itself constantly chang-ing, nowhere can anything like a permanent 'I' be found. No-I is one of the Three Marks of Being, Suffering and Change being the other two. The insight that the Five Aggregates are all inherently empty is all that is necessary. No more is needed to pass beyond suffering. But we do not easily come to it. In order to approach it in a roundabout way, all the Buddhist Teachings, all the twelve divisions of the Canon that fill three huge library rooms, are just elaborations of this one simple fact: the Five Aggregates which make up us human beings are in themselves all empty. Nowhere in them is there anything approaching an I to be found. 'Thus he passed beyond suffering.'

'Oh Sariputra, form is not different from emptiness, emptiness is not different from form. Form is emptiness, emptiness is form.' This is the Buddha himself speaking, or Avalokitesvara, it does not matter. Sariputra was one of the great disciples of the Buddha in the First Turning of the Wheel of the Dharma. In the Hinayana teachings, the Buddha first proclaimed the Four Noble Truths, and all his great disciples came to insight by practising them. Sariputra was one of them. It is not to be taken as polemic but an illustration that the Way goes in stages. So, in these disciples, having come to that first insight – and this can happen to us too – there arises the notion that 'It is all over, now I can settle down. Now I know, I am relieved of the burden that I have been carrying.' But if there is a settling down on it, it very soon begins to change. It will not hold, is not irreversible. So in the Mahayana version the Buddha, having first preached the Four Noble Truths and the coming to insight through them, next taught the Prajna Paramita, proclaiming that the Way goes further, becomes more profound. Some of those who had thought there was no more to be done did not like this. They felt bitterly disappointed and left, but others listened and started anew. That applies to us, too. Do not think that this is a historical fact. In Buddhism we have very little history but we have many allegories and parables. This is very, very important to realize. Looked at with the Great Wisdom Gone Beyond, the thought 'I have got it' is delusion.

'Oh Sariputra'! Sariputra is directly addressed, for he is one who continues training, one who truly listens, a true Sravaka. 'Form is not different from emptiness, emptiness is not different from form.' Is that not a blatant contradiction? Here next to me sits a person; you cannot deny that he has got a form. There he sits, and it is not true that there is no person, you cannot just deny his presence. What is the Prajna Paramita, the Great Wisdom Gone Beyond, telling us? It does not say that there is no form as such. It only says that form is not different from emptiness. You may look at the latest science and conclude it is true that there is no person and that every atom is a whirling mass of neutrons and protons, etc. and they are all whirling in space. Where then is a person? This however, is not meant by the Buddhist Teachings that 'form is not different from emptiness and emptiness is not different from form.'

The Dharma, the way all things really are, is in the Buddhist view the principle or essence which informs all forms, and all forms conform to it, act in accordance to that information. It informs equally the stone or a booklet, an ant and an elephant, each conforming and acting as fits the specific form. An ant will always act as an ant, an elephant as an elephant. This is the wisdom and power of the Tathagata. In spring, flowers appear. They do not say, 'Oh no, the sun has gone and it is beginning to snow. I am remaining at home in the nice warm earth.' When it is their time to come up, they come and unfold themselves. That is the form conforming to that information. We have no word for it because we do not see it like that, we always want to have 'reasons'. All forms, except the human, conform to that inborn information. As the Buddha said, 'All beings are fully endowed with the Tathagata's wisdom and power. But sadly, human beings, because of their attachments are not aware of it.' And our most persistent attachment, the source of all others, is the conviction that 'I am'.

We tend to have much difficulty with the Buddhist concept of No-I and with the statement that 'form is not different from emptiness, emptiness is not different from form'. But think of 'Life' as such, a concept we can think of, but there is no such thing as Life separate and apart from form. We talk about sentient beings and insentient beings. Insentient beings, we believe, have no life, yet they also conform according to their inherent information. Can we see Life itself? No, it is in us, we are it. But can you pull out your life and say, 'This is my life and here it is'? Or can you even point to it? In itself it is nothing. It is just a concept. We think that we understand Life, but we cannot. It lives us. It would keep us in conformity with that inborn information if we would only allow it to do so. However, I, being convinced that I am I, you are you and the table is the table, all separate entities, will not allow this information to become conscious. Perhaps we can listen to the Heart Sutra now.

'Oh Sariputra, form is not different from emptiness, emptiness is not different from form. Form is emptiness, emptiness is form.' The two are inextricably connected. You cannot have one without the other. 'Form is emptiness, emptiness is form.' Seen from one side, it is empty. Seen from the other, it looks like form. But all forms are composites and impermanent, with no fixed identity. We take ourselves so seriously and are so full of clever know-how that we are not capable of looking in a direct way – 'Now I see you, now I don't.'

'Form is emptiness, emptiness is form. The same applies also to feeling or sensation, perception, mental configurations and consciousness.' These are the Five Aggregates that make up a human being: form, the body; feeling or sensation, mental or physical feelings; perception, thoughts, putting labels on things, for example 'This is a table' etc. Then the mental configurations or volitional formations, our habitual notions, the Karmic mass from the past under the compulsion of which we create still further Karma. And finally consciousness, awareness. These are the Five Aggregates, which the Bodhisattva Avalokitesvara saw as all empty and thus passed beyond suffering.

If the Five Aggregates are seen as truly empty, that is the end of suffering. Nothing need be added to that. But since nobody is ever happy with something that is straight and simple, it is emphasised, 'Oh Sariputra, all things are in themselves empty.' Not just that there is no I in this formation or in this form, but that all things (technically called all dharmas) are in themselves empty, 'neither coming to be nor ceasing to be, neither pure nor impure, neither increasing nor decreasing.' You cannot put any labels on them, one way or the other. And so within emptiness there is no form, within real emptiness (Sunyata, to give the Sanskrit term) there is 'no form, no feeling, no perception, no mental configurations, no consciousness.' In other words, the Five Aggregates do not exist in that emptiness. There is just a spacious roominess with nothing swabbling about in it. 'Within emptiness there is no eye, no ear, no nose, no tongue, no body, no mind; there is no field of seeing, of hearing, of smelling, of tasting, of touching, no field of consciousness.'

First of all, we are startled – 'no eye, no ear, no nose, no tongue, no body, no mind...'. But there is a nose, there is an ear – I can touch it! That is within the form, but form is emptiness and emptiness is form. That is where we need to do a jump and declutch. If we have studied Buddhism correctly, these are the basic teachings, the Eighteen Dhatu. And yet here they are denied! 'No eye, no ear' etc., 'no field of seeing, hearing' and so on. No perception either. We are in the second turning of the Wheel, which is the Mahayana, the Great Way.

It goes further. Now we go into the teaching of emptiness. 'Within emptiness there is no delusion nor extinction of delusion, and so on (through the twelve links in the Chain of Dependent Origination).' The whole of the Buddhist teaching seems radically denied. As depicted in the Wheel of Life, the Twelve Links start with basic Delusion and go through Volitional Impulses, Consciousness, Name and Form, the Six Sense Organs, Touch, Feeling/Sensation, Thirst/Craving, Grasping/Clinging, Becoming, Birth to Old Age and Death.

But within emptiness, there are none of these links, and, finally, 'no Old Age and Death and no extinction of Old Age and Death'. We have to look carefully. 'There is no delusion nor extinction of delusion' etc. A delusion, not being there, does not need to be extinguished. Therefore, when we, in our silliness and unknowing, want to get rid of this or that trait, whether inside us or outside, it is all delusory fantasy. All we need is to get ourselves into a state where the seeing is cleared, where the opinions, ideas, convictions and attachments fade away. Where do my opinions come from? Or the conviction that this is a table? We always want to pursue the conviction instead of tracing it back to its root.

Perhaps a useful analogy would be turning on the heating because it is getting cold. We know of heat and cold as such and want to be warm. So we change or try to change the out- side condition to conform to my wants. But there is another possibility, and this is the Buddha's Way. Yes, we know of heat and cold. There is a limit to how much a human body can endure. But the Buddha's Way, rather that trying to change outside conditions, enquires what is it that does not like, does not want to endure. Where does it come from? Why is it loudly clamouring? Into this the Buddhist goes to find out, and thus goes beyond suffering.

If concerned with the outside, then if hot we need a fan, invent air-conditioners, become more and more demanding, more and more wasteful and ever less caring, ever more self-concerned, restless and so ever more driven and unhappy. But if instead of looking outside we question who is wanting, we come to another seeing, another hearing, another smelling etc. where wantings and dislikings no longer reach. So, 'Within emptiness there is no delusion and no extinction of delusion...' Finally, there is no old age and death and no extinction of old age and death because bodies are born, they live for a span, grow old and die. This is a known fact. But do we need to say that 'This is I.'? Do we think that we are the body? Or do we feel that it is my body? I am very concerned about what happens to my body and get perturbed to think that this my body might come to an end. Why? If there is no delusion and only clear seeing of emptiness, then what is the body?

Back to the Five Skandhas. We can do with a closer look at these. The physical one, form or body, is limited, in space and time. The other four are mental. Feeling/sensation informs whether something is pleasant or not, or whether hard or soft.

Next are perceptions or thoughts or labels – table, booklet, person. Then there are volitional or mental conformations or impulses, the fairy tale collection of past Karma colouring all my perceptions, fears, wants and dislikes. They are the distorting mirror through which everything is seen. An Austrian proverb says that at night all cats are black. This Samskara Skandha is also the repository of our moods. If I am in a bad mood, everything looks hopeless or annoying, and when I am cheerful, everything is fine. But when somebody steps on my toe, I am instantly a raging demon, at least inwardly. This is what 'I' am conscious of. Now Buddhism does not say we should do nothing at all, but it teaches the Middle Way. Some situations may be improved/changed without damaging the environment. If there is a toothache, we go to the dentist, etc. But in the immediate here and now, there can be no more than an immediate response, skilful or unskilful and a simple seeing as it is and a simple going with it, that is true consciousness, in which there is no delusion and no extinction of delusion. Old age and death are no longer a worry.

Of these Five Aggregates, when the body/form, being composite, breaks up, which it inevitably will, the four mental strands go on. In the course of the life of one body, this fourfold bundle has changed and will need to find itself a now fitting form. That is also within the way all things really are. In that form, it will also inevitably be more or less altered during the life span of that form, and so on. The Buddhist idea of rebirth comes from that. We always mistake it as something personal, as if the soul goes marching on, but there is no soul in Buddhism. Only this fourfold bundle continues, but is itself constantly changing. 'Impermanent are all compounded forms,' are the Buddha's last words, 'walk on, heedfully.'

'Emptiness is form and form is emptiness' does not deny the forms. It only sees them as quite ephemeral, of no real concern. So, 'Within emptiness there is no suffering, no cause of suffering, no end of suffering and no way to the end of suffering.' We know that this formulation of suffering is another of the great Buddhist teachings, the Four Noble Truths. Here they are also denied and are to be taken merely as formulae that help us to see what is clearly expressed already in the understanding of the Five Skandhas.

'Within emptiness there is no knowledge, no attainment and nothing that can be attained.' That is most upsetting, isn't it? 'Within emptiness there is no knowledge...'. But after all, I do the Buddhist training in order to come to understanding. We are back with 'I' once more. But in the Heart Sutra, the Great Wisdom Gone Beyond, anything that I can cling on to, hold on to, anything that makes me feel 'I', anything that I hope will make me better, greater, more lasting is all neatly pulled out from under my feet. 'Within emptiness there is no knowledge, no attainment and nothing that can be attained.' So what am I doing here, training for what? I could entertain myself better with something else. There is nothing for me to obtain from the Dharma, no 'I' to get any thing and no thing that can be attained. We, with our attachments, will not easily take to that, so we still go wobbling on.

But the Bodhisattva, knowing all this, relies on the Great Wisdom of Emptiness which denies all ideas of I. That is the Great Wisdom Gone Beyond. Not only beyond I but beyond everything. There is nothing but a spacious roominess. However, even a slight approach to that roominess is likely to evoke fear. Those few who have been away from our familiar earth and out into space have all been deeply impressed by this vast emptiness and came back changed. 'The Bodhisattva relies on the Great Wisdom Gone Beyond...', on that vast spaciousness, 'and so his heart is free of hindrances.' If that is seen into, then the hindrances of 'I must have' and 'I won't have' etc. are gone. 'Because his heart is free of hindrances, he is free of fear.' This is the really important message. If there are no hindrances, there can be no fear. If there is no fear, there can be no I, because fear and I, I and fear, are like the palm and the back of the hand. They are inseparable. The Bodhisattva, whose heart is free of hindrances ('I' being the number one hindrance) is also free of fear.

'Going beyond all error and delusion, he enters final Nirvana. All past, present and future Buddhas rely on the Great Wisdom Gone Beyond and so attain to Perfect and Complete Awakening', which is to see things the way they really are. This vision, this great vision, is the great insight. The Heart Sutra, helping us out of being caught up in our small I-ness, continues, 'Know therefore that the Great Wisdom Gone Beyond is the Great Mantra...' A Mantra does not need to have meaning. Being chanted again and again, it imbues the four mental Skandhas to the extent that it also penetrates the form/body, and so all the Five Skandhas, and there is nothing left but this Mantra. The 'Great Wisdom Gone Beyond is the Great Mantra, the Wisdom Mantra...', which really is the life in us rather than mere thoughts in our head. This 'Wisdom Mantra ... is supreme and peerless and delivers from all suffering.' If it is really entered into, even for just moments, a door will have opened. Even if it fades away, by sincere practice this Mantra, 'which is supreme and peerless and delivers from all suffering', can be approached again. And so the Mantra of the Great Wisdom Gone Beyond is proclaimed, 'Gone, Gone, Gone

Beyond, Gone Altogether Beyond, Enlightenment Fulfilled'. If we chant it with a full heart, which is also an empty heart, the Mantra will imperceptibly perfume that bundle which for the time being makes up what foolishly I think to be 'myself'.

The Buddha compared the Five Skandhas to a cart. You can ride in it, know what it is, but taken apart, where then is the cart? So also in the Five Aggregates bundle, no 'I' can be found, and yet, if put together, it works, like the cart works. If full of fancy ideas, it works in an unskilful way, is wasteful of energy and provides a bumpy ride!

The bundle of the Five Aggregates, if left to its own inborn information, will smoothly and peacefully continue, in harmony with the given situation. Such a state of inner harmony is also perceptible to others. This is why the chanting ends with the Vows of dedicating oneself to be of use to others. We cannot be of use to others without profiting ourselves, too. So it is re-union with the inner harmony which has never been absent but which, because of our attachments, we cannot be aware of. The Heart Sutra, if we only listen to it, radically dismantles all attachments. Then, with the heart free of hindrances, there is no fear, 'The heart rolls with the ten thousand things and this rolling is truly mysterious'.

THE DHARANIS AND THE
TRANSMISSION

Dharani of Removing Disasters, Dharani of Adoration

Comments by Venerable Myokyo-ni

We chant these two Dharanis after the Heart Sutra. The Dharani of Removing Disasters is followed by the Dharani of Adoration. Dharanis are perhaps best thought of as composites, meaning Mantra, invocation and spell. They have always been very popular. In whatever religion, we will find something akin to them, the perennial effort to ward off misfortune and the striving for some value that is more than oneself and to which the human heart longs to be lifted up and be re-united with. If that is neglected or forgotten, then only I is left and 'I only' is not enough to fill the heart and satisfy its longing. In times when the religious and cultural values have been lost, we have great difficulty in going beyond I. So instead we feel the need for some 'mission', hence the New Age and fundamentalist movements. Moreover, in our irreligious time we equate the religious sense with superstition and blind faith. Even in our unbelieving days, every five minutes we say or think 'Oh, God!' It is natural that the small 'I' which I am feels the need for some support or some value to hold on to. We do the chanting so that the heart can open up and empty itself of all the fancy ideas that we usually entertain.

We start the morning chanting with the Repentance Sutra and the Going for Refuge to Buddha, Dharma and Sangha. With this we lay the foundation. Then we chant the Heart Sutra for a final 'clearing' – 'no eye, no ear, no nose', etc. – and from that spacious roominess see that in our world there are tragedies, misfortunes and disasters as well as joy and happiness. As we need to hold on to something, we first chant the Dharani of Removing Disasters. Dharanis are not mysterious but they have a mystic quality. If we chant whole-heartedly, a disaster might actually not occur because in chanting wholeheartedly we are whole-hearted also, and so we might see or notice what otherwise we might not become aware of.

I remember that in my later years in Japan, I would in spring and autumn go for a few days to a small island in the Inland Sea. Its south coast was a very high, almost vertical, cliff, with only three small coves going down. The cliff path hugged the winding coast closely and on every sharp turn was a little Jizo, the Bodhisattva who looks after children and travellers. Long being used to such effigies and just automatically bowing on sight, I perfunctorily stopped and bowed, and at that moment I saw that it was a much sharper bend than usual.

I was rather tired, and had I not stopped and bowed I would have gone right over. Shocked and full of gratitude, there was a realization of the value of bowing and of the Dharanis. If we keep that in mind, we might avoid falling into all those difficulties one so easily falls into, be they physical or mental. So with much gratitude and with a full heart, we chant the Dharani of Removing Disasters.

With nothing more to worry us, we can hand ourselves over to gratefully chant the next Dharani, Adoration of the Buddha. Also chanted three times, it expresses Adoration of the Triple Treasure, adoration also of Avalokitesvara whom we know from the Heart Sutra, the Bodhisattva-Mahasattva of great compassion. 'Aum to the one who performs a leap out of all fears! Having adored him, may I enter into the heart of the blue-necked one known as the noble, adorable Avalokitesvara!' And so it goes on.

To the head it is high-falutin language, but when the heart is in it, it lifts up and out of our small littleness into a quite different realm where true religion shines. There we can really see the great Lord Avalokitesvara in his great compassion and we can really bow in front of him. This truly bowing and laying down the heart is the turning point. Soko Roshi once said to me, 'All that is necessary is to lay down the heart, not just the body' and added, 'But it usually takes ten to fifteen years to bring it off.' Chanting the Dharani of Adoration helps us to lay down the heart.

Once we have laid down the heart there is nothing more to fear. We may read in the religious texts that with great faith we can 'walk on water as on dry land'. 'Not possible', say I, taking it literally. But if not afraid, not thinking that I cannot walk on water, then perhaps I would somehow manage to get across quiet water, like a dog or cat. If I could hand myself over truly and trustfully to something that I know will hold and protect me, it is not difficult to see that all my throwing myself about is quite unnecessary and is creating difficulties rather than being of use. From this arises the real willingness to submit, to give over. This is also at the core of all religions, whether of East or West. It is the basis for getting out of the shell that 'I' am and which gets the more crusty and hard the more I feel myself unconnected and separate. 'I' is the basic delusion which is the first link in the Twelve-fold Chain.

When we chant the Dharani of Adoration with its rhythm and really give the heart into it, something will happen. At our

Priory Sesshin, on the last evening we are always invited to Evensong with the nuns. They sing, 'Into Thy Hands, oh Lord, I commend my spirit.' In all difficulties, at times when we do not like something or when something is oppressive or painful, hard and sorrowful to us, if we then can really hand over, 'Into Thy Hands I commend my spirit', whether it is the Lord or Avalokitesvara or whoever, we will find that at that moment there is release and relief, because the burden of 'I' has 'dropped off'.

Soko Roshi told me that soon after Zuigan Roshi had died, he had a visit from an elderly gentleman who had been a disciple of Zuigan Roshi. He was retired, had recently lost his wife, his children were grown up and well off. He himself had been a chamberlain in the Imperial Household. He now had nobody and felt terribly unhappy and lonely, and would Soko Roshi please take him into the temple. Soko Roshi told him that temple life was geared to young people and not suitable for an elderly gentleman. But seeing his desperation, he could not just send him away, clearly he needed something to hold on to, to right himself again. No use to tell him to sit Zazen, for he had spent much of his life attending court proceedings in formal position rigid on his knees from three in the morning onwards. He had done more Zazen than any Zen master! Would the contemplation of nature and its beauty be of help? No, because being educated and used to aesthetic appreciation, when seeing a flower, up would come a verse or poem from the huge Chinese/Japanese poetry collection; he would not just see the flower! 'Finally' Soko Roshi said, 'I told him that when feeling really sad he should go into his innermost room where nobody could see him and there to lay himself down like a little child, to prostrate himself without thinking for what or to whom.'

A month later the gentleman came back looking quite cheerful. 'I am so grateful for your advice. Life has taken on quite a different colour. Will you now take me as your disciple?' Soko Roshi said, 'You look rather happy.' 'Yes,' said he, 'I am happy.' 'But why do you then want to become my disciple?'

It is as simple as that. Nothing but laying down, without ado, like a little child. The head, 'I', may not understand but the body does and the heart does. Little by little we can learn to do it just as we can learn to chant these Dharanis. They also 'work'.

Then we chant the Transmission. If I think only of myself, then I cannot but feel separate in a world that is often other than I would like. But if I know myself as a member of, and at one with, an old family, I am connected, am the latest link in a long chain, contributing my bit to its continuation.

We start not with Buddha Shakyamuni but with the legendary, mystical Buddhas – to remind ourselves that our own world is only a tiny speck in a vast cosmic and temporal system, that there were Buddhas before our own Shakyamuni Buddha and that they all handed down the Dharma. Then there is the Transmission from Shakyamuni Buddha to his disciples in India and China, each walking the Way of the Buddha and so keeping it open, alive.

At the Priory in front of the house is a lawn. There for Sesshin, if we all walk across the lawn to the tennis court, soon the grass is bent and the beginnings of a little path show up. If a path is constantly used, it will become wider, the grass will disappear and it is clearly seen. The more it is used the wider it will become. So it is also with the Buddha's Way.

'Our' Buddha Shakyamuni therefore said that he had only 're-discovered an ancient path'. That path had been overgrown as it often becomes, until a Buddha once more re-discovers it. And he said that this path was leading to an ancient city – the human heart. The Buddha then spent the rest of his long life showing others how to walk that path. And by following his footsteps, his disciples kept it open. With each generation it became clearer and there were more 'maps' of it – the scriptures, becoming ever more detailed, showing up obstacles, here a cliff and there a ravine, a swamp, a raging river and how to deal with each. We do well to acquaint ourselves with the map.

If you look at all the teachings, they speak with one voice, stating exactly the same only in different words, showing up highlights and difficulties. But it is through that long chain of those who actually walked the path and had a disciple who also walked it, that the Way or the 'map', the living teachings, are preserved to this day. It is now up to us whether we are willing also to follow that path or otherwise to lose ourselves in the jungle. If we chant the transmission all the way through, there comes a feeling of being not an individual who hangs unconnected somewhere but who is a link in a chain. That gives us more courage and more determination to continue on the Way, so that our own footsteps, however few, also help to keep that path open for those who come after. So we have the continuous chain all the way from the Buddha linking all who walk it now and carrying forward into the future.

Being linked up like that, the heart opens and we chant with much gratitude. From that derives the strength to keep walking, and so we 'walk on' for the good of others and ourselves. There is no goal to be achieved, no end, and every step is its own reward. 'The Buddha's teaching is lovely in the beginning, lovely in its middle and lovely in its consummation.'

So we chant the Transmission in gratitude to all those old masters who spent their lives walking the Way to keep it open for us who are now doing our own bit. We find ourselves with much gratitude walking the Great Way in which are fused together wisdom and warmth as well as the strength to function out of it, in accord with it.

Elsie Mitchell, who spent some years in Japan, once wrote to me that 'the warmth and the beauty of the Mahayana have not yet been translated.' And it is quite true. We tend to take the teachings intellectually and we do not get the feel of the warmth and the beauty that is in all Buddhism. It is particularly stressed in the Mahayana to open up towards things as they are, to compassionately partake in and contribute to this world as it is. That means taking action in it wisely, which is according to what the circumstances demand and not what I think.

'The heart rolls with the ten-thousand things, this rolling is truly mysterious.' Coming or going, when making tea or drinking tea, just to take part in what is. To do one's job and to conform to what the clear heart-mirror, the Buddha-wisdom, tells us. It is always there, always approachable. Only I tend to misunderstand and/or misuse it, to slant it according to what I like. If we come back to the real, basic teachings, they clearly point the Way. When the longing of the heart is fulfilled, we enter a new landscape, that of the Four Brahma Viharas, the Divine Abodes, 'Divine' because they go beyond I.

The first one is Good-Will, the real warmth of heart that flows freely from the heart. We misunderstand the Buddha's teaching in the Metta Sutta if we think that 'I' have to produce Metta, 'loving kindness', and then have to pump it out like a spray, drenching everything around me. It is ludicrous. How can I? Try to pump out your warmth of heart to somebody whom you dislike! This is the misunderstanding. The more you try, the more convoluted it becomes. Real warmth of heart is the Good-Will that arises of itself when I no longer feel isolated, desperately trying to defend myself. If I feel myself embedded in and at one with everything, there is nothing but Good-Will because there is no thing other than I and no separate 'I' exists. And when there is only Good-Will, it needs no I to pump it, it just flows naturally. The sun does not 'want' to warm us, it just shines. Clouds may seemingly obscure it, but that does not change the sun. It shines because shining is its nature. Whether we seek the sunshine and warmth or go into the shade is our business, it does not concern or offend the sun. This is a helpful analogy which we need to keep in mind. So the first Brahma Vihara is naturally there. It is not blind, does not find sentimental excuses. There is clarity of seeing but no taking issue. So Good-Will can act freely, and can have remarkable effect.

Angulimala had murdered nine hundred and ninety-nine people, and from every victim he had cut off the little finger and made a necklace of them. He swore that his thousandth victim would be the Buddha. As he stole up behind, the Buddha was aware of him and his intention but walked on unperturbed. At the last moment, he turned around and looked at Angulimala in a friendly way with all-pervading Good-Will. Not for nothing is it said that the Buddha had a golden body! When Angulimala saw that great being with no fear at all, only the power of friendliness, he fell down in front of the Buddha, begged his forgiveness and became his disciple.

Yes, it is quite remarkable what true Good-Will can do. Perhaps when we next hear of Metta and that 'I must pump out Metta', we can remember Angulimala and what Good-Will actually entails.

It opens up a truly new world for us, and with this we are embedded in the whole practice, willingly doing the training not just for ourselves but for everybody because, as Master Sesso once said, 'One cannot do this training for oneself alone.' Inevitably, to the extent that it is done, even half a step, it is done not only for oneself but for everybody.

In the concrete awareness of our connectedness, the sense of loneliness, of being separate and exposed is no longer there. So we can peacefully and trustfully walk on, giving ourselves ever more into the walking. We shall find that the more we do so, the easier it gets, the lighter and more joyful and the warmer. The inevitable difficulties that belong to a human life are then looked on not as calamities that happen to me, but as the ordinary ups and downs of life, to be dealt with as well as possible, borne to the extent as must be but without the usual complaints and rather taken as good practice. Yes, passions will still rise while the thought of an 'I' is there and they will try to sweep 'I' away. This can now be seen without being carried away by them. Now the passions are seen as tremendous energy, available to be made use of, to work with them. In this our training, there is nothing that we need to be afraid of, nothing that needs to be refused or rejected. Everything, just as it is, is grist to the mill. In this spirit, things no longer affect us all that much. Only when I feel unconnected, a tiny separate fragment, do I want to overcome things and can I be swept away by a blind wave of passion. If we take that to heart and ponder it carefully, everyday, it will make a lot of difference. Do not feel alone, that is delusion. Only 'I' can think myself alone. Factually, there is only interconnectedness. Ponder this carefully and cultivate that warmth of heart.

DAITO KOKUSHI'S ADMONITION

The National Teacher Daito (1282–1338) admonished his monks, 'All you monks who have come here to this mountain monastery, remember why you are assembled here. You have gathered for the practice of the Way and not for food and clothing. While you have shoulders, you will have clothes to wear and while you have mouths, you will have food to eat. Throughout the twelve periods of the day, devote yourselves unceasingly to the perception of the Inconceivable. Time flies like an arrow. Be reverent, do not allow your hearts to chase after the manifold. Take heed, take heed!

After my pilgrimage (death) you might be incumbents of richly endowed temples, towers and halls, with Sutra books inlaid with gold and silver, and devotees crowding all around.

Or you may chant Sutras and Dharanis, sit in meditation for long hours without sleep, eat but one meal a day and keep all the religious observances throughout the six periods. But unless in your heart you truly dwell on the wonderful Way that cannot be transmitted by Buddha and Patriarchs, you will fail to bring forth the fruit and cause the downfall of the true line. Such as these belong to the family of evil spirits and may not call themselves my descendants, no matter how long ago I have departed from this world. But if there is just one person, even if living in remote wilderness in a hut thatched with just one bundle of reeds and eating wild plants and roots cooked in a pot with a broken leg, if only he whole-heartedly applies himself to investigate and clarify the One Great Matter, he sees me face to face every day and requites his debt of gratitude. Who would dare to despise such a one? Be diligent, be diligent!'

Comments by Venerable Myokyo-ni

The chanting of the Transmission is followed by Daito Kokushi's Admonition in old Japanese. The above translation reminds us of what it is about and gives depth to our chanting. The National Teacher ('Kokushi') Daito, founder of Daitoku-ji, is particularly close to us because we follow his line. On his deathbed he admonished his monks to be diligent in their practice.

Daito Kokushi started his religious life quite early. He had a crippled leg and could not sit properly. We usually learn to meditate balanced on a cushion. But although the body certainly has to come into it, it is not a question of the body only. If it is truly not possible, Zazen can be done in other ways too. The strength that accrues from diligent practice is illustrated by Daito Kokushi on his deathbed. Like most of the great teachers, knowing his end was near and with his disciples around him, he wrote his death poem and addressed his disciples, as above.

Then, at the moment of dying, he grabbed his crippled leg, 'All my life I have been obedient of you, but now you will obey me,' wrenched it up into Zazen posture and with blood spurting out, died. His bloodstained robe is kept in Daitoku-ji to this day, and is always displayed on the twenty-second of November, the anniversary of his death.

Gruesome? Or showing the great strength of fearlessness that accrues from long and diligent practice? In our irreligious and I-orientated time we are no longer acquainted with the sensation of awe – the awareness of something transcending and sublime. But the religious life cannot be lived without that. In Christianity, too, whenever a heavenly messenger approaches a mortal, it is inevitably with the words, 'Fear not!' Have we ever wondered why and what this means? That is what is shown in that gesture.

How much do we want to do this training? What does it really mean to us? What do we want to get from it and what are we willing to give for it? Many of the great stories illustrate just that. Eka, who became Bodhidharma's heir, hacked off his arm. Ummon's leg got crushed. These may be just stories but they are to the point. Are we willing to give that much or do we just expect to get something, playing at it and hoping that something will happen? It is not surprising that then nothing comes out of it. After twenty years doing the practice, perhaps a bit has changed, but not much.

That does not mean we should now go and hack off an arm. That would be merely foolish. But would we be willing to slice off a bit of the little finger of our left hand and offer that up?

So we gratefully remember the National Teacher Daito, founder of Daitoku-ji. Two Japanese emperors were his disciples. One gave him the land on which now Daitoku-ji stands.

'All you monks who have come here to this mountain monastery' – though this was said to his monks, do not think that he addresses just them or only the students of that time.

He also speaks directly to us. 'All you monks who have come here to this mountain monastery'. Daitoku-ji is not built on a mountain; it is on the flat, on the 'Purple Plains'. But from their beginning in China, Zen monasteries were founded mostly on mountain tops in remote areas, and for this reason a Zen monastery to this very day is said to be 'on a mountain'. The big gate that leads to the enclosed compound of the monastery is always called the Mountain Gate.

Daito Kokushi then continues, and speaks to all of us, 'Remember why you are assembled here. You have gathered for the practice of the Way, and not for food and clothing.' And so, if we, too, really keep to the practice of the Way, then everything we encounter, pleasant, unpleasant or indifferent, is grist to the mill. It is all offered for the practice of the Way, and so can be made use of as the practice of the Way. Master Daito tells his monks that while they have shoulders they will have clothes to wear and there will be food to eat. It is as simple as that. Just food to eat, and clothes to wear that is all, no picking or choosing.

With the day divided into two-hour periods, the twelve periods of the day include both the day's active periods and the night periods. Do not slacken 'throughout the twelve periods of the day'. Even asleep, even in your dreams, 'devote yourself unceasingly to the perception of the Inconceivable.' The Sixth Patriarch calls it the True Nature. It is inconceivable to me, cannot be understood, cannot be grasped yet it is the perception that radiates from everything. An old master said, 'I look at the flower, and the flower looks at me.' That is not 'my' perception analysing that 'This flower is red, how nice, so early in spring, I like it' or however we judge and discriminate. No, the perception of the inconceivable is to see/perceive the flower just as it is – in its uniqueness it radiates the inconceivable.

Master Daito then warns us, 'Time flies like an arrow. Be reverent. Do not allow your hearts to chase after the manifold.' We tend to procrastinate. At this moment, it is rather inconvenient. Tomorrow, in five minutes, or whatever excuse we invent. But time flies like an arrow and unless done now, there may not be another chance. Life, too, flies like an arrow and is quickly over. Now we have the precious good fortune to be born as a human being with a human body. The teachings tell us that out of the six destinies, only from the human state is deliverance possible, and that it takes a long time until such an auspicious birth can come to be. And now we are human beings, are we sure we are not frittering away the time and then suddenly die? And what then? We might not come back into the human state, might have lost this precious, rare opportunity simply by procrastination.

Not only that. Four things, it is said, are necessary in order to be able to enter the Way. The first is to be born as a human being. But there are long periods of time in which awareness of the Buddha Dharma has died out. Then a new world age comes and with it a new Buddha. So second it is necessary to be born at such a time when the Buddha Dharma exists. Number three is to be born at a place where it exists. If we had been born two hundred years ago here, we would not have heard anything about the Buddha Dharma. So it is essential to be born at a time and a place where it exists. And finally, we must come into contact with it and incline towards it. These are the four auspicious things: birth as a human being; to live at a time of the existence of the Buddha Dharma; to live at a place of the existence of the Buddha Dharma; and to actually come into contact with it and to be so touched that we are inspired to enter the Way.

We who are reading this have all four conditions fulfilled. Time flies like an arrow. Are we reverent? Do we ever consider what reverence really means? In our irreligious Ice Age, we have lost that feeling, and we need to foster it again, because without being reverent, without being willing to bow, we cannot re-enter wholeness. We feel separate and so cannot care. Lifting and setting down the smallest thing reverently is not our habit, is it? And yet we need to recall that, for there is the entrance.

Years ago we had a monk staying for a few days with a certain member of the group. He was keen to have his flat spick and span with everything ordered to the exact angle. The monk offered to dust while he went to work but he almost shrieked, 'No, no, do not touch anything!' for he was sure all would be left awry. But when he came home, he found the flat perfectly dusted with not one object even one degree out of place. That is what is called working reverently with everything that comes, and it is impressive.

We have grown careless through lack of reverence. Whenever a room is dusted, even in our training temples, there are traces, corners forgotten, objects misplaced. Do you know the story of the tortoise? It did not want to leave traces of its feet in the sand and used its tail to wipe them out, so leaving a huge trail behind. Are we doing the same?

'Be reverent', says Daito Kokushi, 'be reverent!' And what is more, if we begin not to take ourselves as the hub and centre of the universe and rather to see all things as Buddha things, will we then also handle them carelessly, lovelessly? We tend to moan nowadays, about lack of relationships, or alienation or whatever. We do not need to moan about it, we just hold ourselves separate and only want rather than reverently give. 'Be reverent. Do not allow your hearts to chase after the manifold,' says Daito Kokushi and continues, 'Take heed, take heed!' 'After my pilgrimage' means after I have finished my pilgrimage through this life, after I have died. 'After my pilgrimage, you might become incumbents of richly endowed temples, towers and halls, with Sutra books inlaid with gold and silver, and devotees crowding all around.' In other words, monks might become the incumbents of richly endowed temples, as indeed many of them were in his time, and not only in his. But in growing rich or well known with many devotees all around, how easy it is to begin to feel like the cat's whiskers, and at that moment the power devil swallows us. Even if to begin with one has started on the right lines, with expansion further and further, slowly one begins to feel that one is something special. And because this wanting to be something special also fills the inborn wish of I, naturally I comes back with a vengeance, sleek and fit. This is what Daito Kokushi warns against. Even as the incumbent of an enormously rich temple and with a large following, do not let your head become swollen. There are many traps into which one can fall.

'Or you may chant sutras and Dharanis, sit in meditation for long hours without sleep, eat but one meal a day and keep all the religious observances throughout the six periods'. The keeping of these observances goes for the light day period, meditation is for the night. All are legitimate training means. We need to study the sutras to have a framework for our training, otherwise we certainly go wrong. Chanting is an equally important part of the training because it empties the heart. Nor can we do without meditation. But Daito Kokushi says that even if we 'sit in meditation for long hours without sleep, eat but one meal a day and keep all the religious observances throughout the six periods', that alone is of no avail for what is important is the heart inclining to the Way. Why so? If there is an intention of getting something from it, that makes it go wrong. And also, if stubbornly, blindly practised because 'I want', it gets rigid, the means become the end and the Way is forgotten. An Indian story illustrates this. A man has been sitting in the forest for years, meditating and calling, 'Krishna, Krishna, when will you come and liberate me? Krishna, Krishna, when will you come and liberate me?' After many years, Krishna came to set him free. He silently approached from behind, laid a hand on his shoulder and had already opened his mouth to speak when the meditator angrily slewed round. 'Don't you see I'm meditating?' Krishna pulled his hand back and walked quietly away.

In our own Zen tradition there is a story of the young monk who became the Great Master Baso Doitsu. He was very eager, thinking that if only he sat long and hard enough, then somehow he would attain insight. It is a common mistake of the beginner, then as now. His teacher realized he was a very promising youngster in need of advice. So one day when he saw him sitting Zazen in a corner, he took up a tile, sat down beside him, started rubbing it and asked, 'What are you doing here?' The young man, very pleased, said, 'I'm meditating to become a Buddha.' The teacher just went on rubbing his tile. The young man said, 'Master, and what are you doing?' 'I'm making a mirror.' 'But no amount of rubbing can make a mirror out of a tile.' 'And no amount of sitting can make a Buddha out of a clod.'

Back in the 1950s, when little was known about Zen training, this story was often considered as denying the importance of meditation in Zen life, thus showing how insufficient information leads to much misunderstanding. But conversely, to sit endlessly for the purpose of gaining something does not do either. Intention has always purpose behind it. Hence, 'All intention misses the target.' A Chinese saying puts it that, 'For the wrong man, even the right means work wrong; for the right man, even the wrong means work right.' However we may look, actually so it is. The right person makes use of what is. To stick blindly, intentionally to something does not answer. Master Daito says, 'Unless in your heart you truly dwell on the wonderful Way that cannot be transmitted by Buddha and Patriarchs, you will fail to bring forth the fruit and cause the downfall of the true line.' Bodhidharma called that wonderful Way that cannot be transmitted, cannot be put into words, 'A special transmission outside the teachings, not standing on written words and letters'. Not even the Buddha could put it into words, all he did was point towards it. 'Buddhas only point the Way.' 'Unless in your heart, you truly dwell on the wonderful Way'. This Way can be walked but it cannot be seen. Is it a Way? In a way it is, and in a way it isn't. It is the way all things really are. And that 'cannot be transmitted by Buddha and Patriarchs'. Only if the heart truly dwells on it can it be followed and lived. If in our hearts we truly dwell on something, then actually we are making that our own; we become it. And so also if we truly in our heart dwell on that wonderful Way, we do not need to try to keep it in mind. We cannot forget it even if we tried. How then could we get away from it?

The Buddha did not say of this wonderful Way that it was something new, only that he had 're-discovered an Ancient Way.' But from his time on, this Way has been followed and so remains open and known. Of all those who have walked it, none has ever said that it was easy, but none has ever said that walking this wonderful Way was not immensely worthwhile. We can still follow it today, and by our own walking the awareness arises that it 'cannot be transmitted by Buddha and Patriarchs'.

Unless we ourselves do the walking and give ourselves wholly into it, the National Teacher Daito warns us that, 'You will fail to bring forth the fruit (not come to that insight) and cause the downfall of the true line.' Once it is forgotten, or neglected, or belittled, the Way becomes overgrown and is difficult to find again, causing 'the downfall of the true line'. Master Daito says, 'Such as these belong to the family of evil spirits and may not call themselves my descendants, no matter how long ago I have departed from this world. But if there is just one person, even if living in a remote wilderness in a hut thatched with but one bundle of reeds, eating wild plants and roots cooked in a pot with a broken leg' – he may live far out in the sticks, in a leaky cottage, collecting wild plants and roots, cooking them in his only pot which has a leg broken off and any moment is likely to spring a leak. His is a totally impoverished life, with nothing to show for. And yet, says Daito Kokushi, 'if he but whole-heartedly applies himself to investigate and clarify the One Great Matter, he sees me face to face every day and requites his debt of gratitude.'

But do not mistake the Great Matter. Master Daito does not say that one who has a rich temple is no good and that only living in utter poverty is the right thing. That would merely be another set of opinions and far from what Daito Kokushi means. It is not the outer circumstances but the heart dwelling on the Way which counts.

An Indian training story tells of a man who went into the forest and at some distance from the village settled down as a recluse. The villagers saw him as a holy man and brought him food. One day, a little kitten came along. He gave it some of his food and the kitten stayed with him. But in the way of kittens, whenever he started to meditate, the kitten climbed all over him, wanting attention. So he made a grass collar and a leash, and whenever he started meditating he tied the kitten next to him, quite close but so that it could not climb up. His fame as a holy man grew and a few young men joined him, hoping that he would teach them and share his wisdom with them. He did not say very much, but they noticed that whenever he was meditating he had his kitten tied up next to him. Soon enough, each one of them had got himself a kitten, had made a leash for it and tied it up. No doubt they began speculating about what type of kitten was the most effective, or what colour, or which kind of leash etc.

I remember the late Trevor Leggett mentioning that a teacher's slightest mistake or some idiosyncrasy is picked up by everybody as if they had been waiting for it, much quicker than the correct moves. And any little mannerism is also imitated at once. We hang on to such things, they 'stand out' and we think them important. It is not true, they are beside the point, not helpful.

One can walk the Way in a rich temple as well as in the woods. It does not depend on the circumstances, what counts is to live whole-heartedly. Some may prefer to stay in a town temple and others will be drawn to a solitary life. In our egalitarian age, we do not realize how much we differ from each other. Despite all women's liberation, women just are different from men by nature, and by nature mountains are high and valleys are deep. They are different by nature, by what they are, not because one is better than the other. This is what we come to realize when the Buddha-eye begins to open. It sees differences but does not evaluate or label. It is not true that everything is the same and that the mugger is as good as the saint. But there is no attempt to exterminate the other. We live in a world which has both light and darkness, night and day. To try to get rid of night, or of day, is merely silly. But we, contrary as we are, in the evening have the lights on until all hours, and in the morning we sleep until the sun is well in the sky. Yet we can't really change the world. Nonetheless even under the worst circumstances, it is possible to keep the heart dwelling on the wonders of the Great Way, and it is also possible not to become proud when circumstances are good. 'Even the finest cashmere jumper you wear, a sheep has worn it before you.' It is quite useful to remind ourselves of this, to take ourselves down a peg and, whenever the nose goes up, carefully to put it right down onto the grindstone again.

'If only he whole-heartedly applies himself to investigate and clarify the One Great Matter...'. We always try to find reasons for everything. But just as we are all different in a way, so we also share certain traits. We may want different things but we all want! Children born by the same parents, brought up in the same home under exactly the same circumstances, turn out different one from the other. 'Stick to the root, do not bother about the branches.'

'Investigate and clarify the One Great Matter,' the matter of life and death, the matter of where we come from and where we are going. When all is said and done, the thing that every I fears is my dissolution, which means my death. Naturally, because to me that is the end. A favourite analogy for the One Great Matter is ocean and waves – the wave is the ocean, and has never been anything but the ocean. However differently shaped from all the other waves, each one of them is but ocean, the One Great Matter. But to really feel and live out of that Oneness takes genuine insight.

Master Daito does not say 'has really seen into it'. He only says, 'if only he whole-heartedly applies himself to investigate and clarify the One Great Matter'. In whole-heartedly applying oneself and investigating, actually we are already there though we do not know it. It could be said that it is already seen into, though we do not know it. Master Daito therefore does not say that this insight is possible only at the very end. As long as the heart is truly in it, every step of that investigation is its own reward and more is not asked. There is no aim, no goal to be reached, no 'now I get rid of the foolishness of life'. There is just whole-hearted applying oneself to investigating and clarifying the One Great Matter – that in itself is it.

When the heart is collected in itself, there is nothing more to be said. There is no before and after, no top and no bottom or anything. And so, who 'whole-heartedly applies himself to investigate and clarify the One Great Matter, he sees me face to face every day and requites his debt of gratitude'. He is at one with me, every day. And in just this whole-heartedly applying, he requites his debt of gratitude, gratitude for having been shown the Way, and gratitude to those who trod the Way before and so kept it open. 'Who would dare to despise such a one?' Even if he were in rags! This one is also the one pictured in number ten of the Bull-Herding Pictures. There he stands, his robe all anyhow, his appearance not correct, but he looks big! Not that he has grown physically – that is not what is meant by it. Somebody who really has come face to face with that One Great Matter has real stature and could not be overlooked – he stands out. This oneness is the spiritual aspect and is the longing of our own heart, longing for reunion with it, and only by and in this reunion is the longing of the heart stilled. Then the heart plays with the circumstances, assisting all sentient beings, and not only sentient beings but all beings. And so Daito Kokushi ends with 'Be diligent, be diligent!'

THE FOUR GREAT VOWS

Sentient beings are numberless, I vow to benefit them all.
The afflicting passions are inexhaustible, I vow to end them all.
The Dharma teachings are manifold, I vow to learn them all.
The Buddha Way is supreme, I vow to go it to the end.

Comments by Venerable Myokyo-ni

The Four Great Vows are chanted in every Zen monastery at least twice a day, morning and evening. They are also chanted after Zazen, after Teisho and after other ceremonies and observances. After each chanting and also at other observances, the merit of it is offered to Buddha, Bodhisattvas and all Beings – nothing is ever kept for ourselves only. Whatever we have gained in our training is handed over to benefit others.

Of these Four Great Vows, the first one is 'Sentient beings are numberless, I vow to benefit them all.' If I vow to be of benefit to all, I am in a rather fortunate position because I have no time to think of myself. At that, I am already fully liberated from the heavy burden of I! But if I do not take these vows seriously and allow myself time to ghost about as usual, then it is not so easy. So it is important to really look at what these seemingly simple four lines actually encompass.

But I can also think, 'Oh no, that's far too much. How can anybody vow to really benefit all sentient beings? It is not possible. If I vow it, then I'm beholden to keep the vow. How can I possibly? No, that's not for me.' But this is not what the Four

Great Vows are about. Of course I cannot do it. Nobody says that I can do it. But if I nevertheless dedicate myself to doing it, that constellates helpful forces. With that we enter the field of religion. Although knowing I cannot do it, yet giving myself with whole heart into it, whether it is keeping the vow or following the Practice, provided I do what I can as wholeheartedly as possible, more is not asked. If I keep on just doing this, then it seems that from the other side comes a helping hand which begins to pull when I can no longer, and that widens out to all sentient beings.

But if I only think of far-ahead goals and forget the Daily Life Practice here in the ordinary daily life with all its little ups and downs, then inner strength cannot develop and nothing will ever come out of it except a strengthening of I. So we need to ponder very carefully. Buddhism is a religion, and in our irreligious age we have forgotten what a religion actually is about – to reunite us again with what we truly are, to that ground from which we all come and return to. Once this begins really to be seen into, then fear also dwindles because I and fear are inseparable, like palm and back of the hand. Whenever I am belittled, touched on my weak point, diminished, up in defence roars the old survival instinct, the whole elementary strength and energy. But if there is no such I left, if it is all gone, handed over to the other side, then that primitive fear is also no longer there. The realization of that ground to which we all belong takes away the fear, and the heart is fulfilled in that realization.

'Sentient beings are numberless, I vow to benefit them all.' That includes me because I am also one of them. Ramana Maharshi was once asked by a great scholar what would happen if the Self was really seen into. The Maharshi said, 'My son, if the

Self is realized, there are no others.' There are no others – we are in the realm of the Kegon Sutra, 'One is all and all is one, one in all and all in one!' That does not say that all is seen as the same. The seeing is very clear, a spoon is a spoon and a cat is a cat. They are different but not 'other'. With that, there is unity again and we understand each other in a quite different way. We often, as an I, have the fancy idea that I understand you, for example. I may have known you for a long time, and in any case the body flashes all kinds of signals. So I think I really understand you, I know what you are thinking. But do I? I may 'understand' or feel whether you are happy or depressed or the like but to really understand your thinking and deliberations is not possible. Even between husband and wife it is rarely possible.

We are individually very different from each other, but that does not mean that we are separate. If you look at a tree in summer with its thousands of leaves, you will not find even two leaves that are exactly the same. But there is no doubt that each particular leaf from, for example, an oak tree is unmistakably that of an oak tree. It is useful to keep things such as this in mind. Each oak leaf, and not only from this oak tree, but from all oak trees, is unique in its individual form, yet at the same time proclaims its inherent 'oakness'. That perhaps serves as a pointer about what being reunited with our own ground, with our own humanity, implies, and not just with our own humanity but with our living being-ness, with our being alive.

With this insight we are not only liberated from the loneliness and terror of our separateness but are also back in harmony with everything that is. In the Tao Te Ching, at the end of the twenty-fifth verse, it says, 'Man obeys the laws of the earth. Earth obeys the laws of heaven. Heaven obeys the laws of Tao.

And Tao obeys its own inherent nature.' When that harmony is once more re-established, then, 'The heart rolls with the Ten Thousand Things. This rolling is truly mysterious.' That is the harmony of being 'at one' with what is, with the Dharma. It informs all forms, and all forms conform to it. In our case, it expresses itself in conformity with being human, and this natural obedience goes harmoniously all the way, at one with the Tao. Being human, it does so in a specific human manner, not in the manner of a lion, not in that of a louse, nor as a fighting demons or hungry ghost.

In our 'individual', cluttered and I-deluded manner, we have the ideal of having to be good. But even if I try to be good, and we certainly all want to be good and have wanted to be good since we were three-year-olds, we have not always brought it off, have we? Neither as children nor nowadays. Not at least in the full Buddhist way, in act, word and thought. Saint Augustine thanked his God that though he made him responsible for his acts, words and thoughts, at least he did not hold him responsible for his dreams.

If reunited with the human state (not-'I'), we do not need to try to be good, we cannot but be good, cannot act other than human, just as an ant will always act and behave as an ant. We do not expect that a tiger will feed on grass. So it is important to understand the nature of different beings or we cannot benefit them. That true understanding comes from the unity, the oneness.

The nature of mountains is to be high. Children by nature are playful and naughty, that is quite 'natural'. This is understanding the differences, but without making a separation and without judgement – who is better, more precious. In our world in which we live, by nature there is darkness and light. Now the sun shines; this morning it rained. Now it is day, soon it will be night. That is the nature of our world and it is no good resisting, stemming ourselves against it, rather making use of it gratefully and going with it for the sake of all beings.

So already in that first line of the Four Great Vows there is much to give us thought. 'Sentient beings are numberless, I vow to benefit them all.' But if there are no others and if what I think of I is also unreal, then all of us have benefited. I remember Sesso Roshi saying to me, 'Of course, one cannot do this training for oneself alone.' Truly not, because the further one goes, the more it opens up and the more inclusive it becomes. That is the numberlessness in which we ourselves as 'I' are extinguished and thus find what we really are.

The next line is, 'The afflicting passions are inexhaustible, I vow to end them all.' We know the three main strands of the afflicting passions as the Three Fires, also called the Three Poisons: delusion, desire and aversion. They sound rather cool and abstract, don't they? But if they have got us really in their grip, they are hot, and overwhelmingly powerful. So we do well to carefully inquire into them. In Buddhist psychology they are divided and classified, and present-day psychology is also concerned with them.

They are in every human being, as long as there is a sense of a separate 'I'. Mahayana teaches that the passions are the Buddha-nature and the Buddha-nature is the passions. That is to say that the same energy is at play but not in the sense that I can now let it all rip and in this am showing my Buddha-nature. On the contrary!

As said above, whenever I am even slightly scratched, there is a fierce reaction. If something happens to me, then I react strongly, even over-react, making a mountain out of a molehill. Why? Because when I feel threatened, fear comes up. Now if we look at the afflicting passions, as long as the delusion of a separate 'I' is there, I wants more, want to have or to get rid of. It is inexhaustible because what I really want is to make myself totally secure, and yet underneath there is a dim intimation that it is impossible. That is Dukkha, usually translated as 'suffering', the basic insecurity of I facing everything else that is other than I. I cannot help it but must labour to make myself as secure as possible, to get ever more of what I want and ever less of what I do not want. But it is labour in vain and I only get more and more stressed.

Inquiring carefully, I find that in the world as it is, with other people and other living beings, everything seems to threaten me because it can and often does interfere with what I like.

So I try two ways. First, I 'want' – to get, make mine, to swallow and 'incorporate' whatever is possible. That is what desire is, to make it mine. What I have swallowed has become 'me', it cannot threaten me any more. So I go on trying to 'make mine'. Fortunately, this does not go very far. All the afflicting passions end in tragedy and calamity. Trying to swallow everything to feel secure will soon explode me.

The other way, I wanting to get rid of, is the same. Both liking and loathing come from fear, and we need to be aware of that. There is the wanting, to swallow and make mine and the other is disliking, wanting to get rid of or to keep out. We all know that feeling. If somebody really annoys us, or even if it is something that just keeps on niggling us, what I really want is to annihilate it. We may decently put some layers over it and say, 'No, I don't really want to, I just would like to get rid of it for a little bit.' But really this is not so. I want to eliminate, instantly. If I have no compunction, I say, 'Ah, look at you, you have always been a thorn in my side' (and at that moment I really believe it although we have been friends for many years!) So I hit out and Ah! The world is now a better place without you. Now I can go on peacefully and peace will be upon all of us. Until someone else annoys me, so he is dispatched, the world again being a better place without him. But soon, the next one annoys to be eliminated too, and so it goes on.

It is always with the same heart-felt, 'Thanks goodness, now the world is a better place, all is well again.' But as a matter of fact, what happens is that my irritations and my having to hit out come more and more frequently because giving into those flashes, my bearing strength of tolerating annoyances atrophies. So I hit out ever more often, and the logical conclusion is that eventually I would find myself in a world in which I am alone, as everything else has been exterminated. But I am now at a fever pitch of irritation, and cannot contain myself. So with nothing left to hit, I explode. Yes, the afflicting passions afflict us, and they grow dangerous if we give in to them. So it is important at least to learn to endure their presence without being carried away by them. Which is very different from our usual habit of repressing them.

Both desire and aversion arise from the same root, fear. Fear is the other side of I, it flares when I feel threatened or cannot have what I want. So we look again at the Three Signs of Being, that everything changes and there is suffering because of I. One of the Three Fires is delusion or ignorance. I do not think of delusion as a Fire. Test it! I and fear are like back and palm of the hand. If I am threatened one way or the other, it is from that I/fear that I react, but that I/fear is delusion, that of being a separate I. And so both turn on the great teaching of No-I, which most of us, and particularly we Westerners, do not understand. All kinds of evasive explanations are bandied about, such as 'He didn't really mean I. Of course there is an I.' I have heard even Eastern teachers say that, because most pander to our Western minds.

Yet it is repeatedly stated in the Buddhist scriptures, they make a clear point of it. Best known is the analogy of a cart or think of a car. You can ride in it but if you take it apart, wheels, axle, driving wheel, shaft and seats and lay it all out side by side, where is the car then? Can you ride home in it? And so we have the teaching of the Five Skandhas, to make that point clear. But rarely do we really ponder those Five Skandhas. It comes a bit too close to dethroning 'Number One', I!

There is the body. There are feelings and sensations, physical and mental. There are thoughts, perceptions. There are volitional conformations which result from past experiences and which form/are the Karma-producing agents. Finally, there is consciousness that belongs to each of the senses. And that is all there is, that bundle of five strands. Nowhere is there an I to be found. Yet that bundle works perfectly, is beautifully attuned to every situation. I cannot nearly achieve such perfect functioning as the bundle, left to itself, does.

But when the delusion of I arises, I having to defend myself, drive myself madly from one difficulty into another, and to run away from myself, react violently, desperately wanting what I cannot have. That is suffering. The Buddha described it as, 'Having what one does not like is suffering. Not having what one does like is suffering. Being parted from what one likes is suffering. Being loaded with what one does not like is suffering. This makes up all the large sum of suffering.'

It is true and we know it 'in cold blood'. But when 'fired', I get the most unrealistic, odd ideas of what I like or can't have. Reason cannot function in the presence of the Fires. For example, I desperately want to go to Greece to see the spring flowers. But, if I really so desperately wanted, why do I not go? Why must I allow myself to be chained here with far too much to do? Why can't I just walk out – with a game leg? And so when realistically pondering the alternatives – what becomes of me if I give in to my unrealistic desire? And I discover that where I actually am is the most acceptable place in the given circumstances! If I really dislike it so much, I can leave. If I do not it means that every other alternative is even less acceptable! I am already in the 'best' place! End of wanting, peace of heart. So to repeat, what I refuse to accept is that as the circumstances are, it is simply in any case not possible for me, for if I so much wanted to go, I would be there at this moment and not sitting here moaning. The fact of my being here already shows that I can't be there. In my imagination I can roam over the three periods of time but factually I am bound by the situation as it is.

Within that situation, there is a certain amount of freedom. But if you look within the situation and that certain amount of freedom, you will find that under the conditions as they are, I have already chosen, without my quite knowing it, the place where I most like to be because every other possibility would not be quite so acceptable as the one that I am anyway in. And so instead of complaining that I cannot have what I want, I realize that as situations go – and we are bound by the situation – I am in any case in the place where I most like to be. And when I then look round and see others are in much worse conditions, there arises compassion instead of just the passion of 'I want, I must'.

'The afflicting passions are inexhaustible, I vow to end them all.' How to do that? I cannot cut them off because they are stronger than I. But it is possible to refuse to give in to them. I can train myself to a great extent, but it is a fine point. If I really force myself to be quite cool, not to feel upset by anything and believe that I have the passions well under control, then sooner or later out of the blue something may happen that really makes the fires flare up again, full blast. What has gone wrong is that it has all been I-induced and grim, the compassionate side has not been awakened.

There is a Zen story, very useful for those in training but misunderstood by others. A monk came begging to an old but well-to-do lady's house. She invited him to stay and would look after his needs, thus ensuring good fortune. So up on the hill she built him a little hermitage, sent up food every day and the monk settled himself down and was very diligent in his religious practices. That went on for some years. Then the old lady began to wonder how the monk was getting on. She told her niece, a pretty girl, 'Today, it's you who bring the food up to him. You put the food on the table, then go up to him, give him a big hug and run straight back to me and tell me what he did.' The girl came back quite shaken, 'I tried with all friendliness to give him a big hug, and he roughly pushed me back, glared at me and said, "For the last two years, there has been no sap in that dry trunk!" Upon which the old lady stormed up the mountain, burnt the hermitage and drove him out. 'If I had known that you were such a one, I would not have kept you for years!'

Now what does that mean? It seems that the dry trunk was artificial, and underneath was growing up something very unpleasant, ready to burst out sooner or later. If he really had been free, he would have smiled at the girl and with a little hug told her, 'Now, now, girlie, you'd better go home again.' That is where true compassion and understanding comes in and with that the real freedom. Does that makes sense? Instead of the rough response caused by repression of what threatens from underneath and that hurts others, too.

There is also the story of the two monks who came to a ford. The water was high and a girl in her finery was hesitating to cross. One of the monks took her on his back, carried her across and put her down on the other side. The two walked on, one scolding the other that this was against the rules. The monk who had carried the girl finally cut in, 'Now, just stop. I put her down the other side but you are still carrying her.' It is useful to remember such stories.

But then how can these afflicting passions be brought to an end? In themselves they carry the full force of life, the basic energy that is in everything, animate as well as inanimate. Hence the Mahayana saying that the Buddha-nature is the passions and vice versa. 'I' am the switch that turns the wisdom and power of the Tathagata into conflagration by my delusion of being separate, different from you and everything, and therefore insecure. It is I who turn it into wants and aversions. If I am in the grip of the delusion of being I, blindly wanting and hating and therefore swayed by that energy which is stronger than I, what can I do? I am carried away by it as usual.

Is there another way to look at and realize the tremendous strength of it? The Buddha's great message is 'Suffering I teach and the way out of suffering.' By admitting that this strength is not 'mine' and willingly handing myself into it, its power will consume me and so end the I-delusion. Where there is no I, there are no more afflicting passions. Then the energy works freely again, choicelessly in changing situations, and has re-become what it always has been, the Buddha-nature.

So in our training we have two possibilities of learning to give ourselves into the Fires. We can start with little things, giving ourselves into what at this moment is being done. But it has to be whole-hearted, even ninety-nine percent cuts no ice. For that purpose we need to learn to pull ourselves together and to jump into the conflagration. It does not go at once. So first of all we start with getting used to the Daily Life Practice and the time-table. Then we can make a survey of how often in the ordinary day tiny reactions of 'No' flare up.

They arise in the body. If we are 'at home' instead of grazing all over the three dimensions of time, we notice the arisings. At that moment we say 'Yes' to it. Normally, we do not want to bother with them, ignore them as not important, 'I can deal with those easily.' But 'my problem' is usually made up of all the little unrecognised and unlived No's that I do not really know.

All those little No's need now to be worked with, every single one. And every time, we must give a conscious 'Yes'. Why are we unwilling to recognise, admit those little 'No's'? We just don't want to realize them. They frighten us, because 'I' must feel in control and those little flurries obstruct me. Now we begin to realize that we are much less in control than we think we are and that many other things influence our behaviour.

That is how we begin. Slowly, we get used to it. 'Instead of learning, get used to it', is a Zen saying. Once we are really used to the little ones, we can take up the medium–sized 'problems' (No's) which so far we just had to endure without being swept away by them. Now we confront these mediumsized flares, and in meeting them we metaphorically fold our hands and bow deeply, 'Precious energy, I am still here. Please burn me away.' Energy in itself is precious. So we open up and let it burn, willingly enduring the emotional onslaught, living it without, however, saying, 'Today I am not going to the office, I have to let the energy burn me away.' That is not on!

So then slowly things begin to shift. We also begin to discover that things go quite smoothly without I interfering. And what is more, suddenly we begin to find that the energy, if it is really given house-room and if really lived, is becoming more amenable, more human. This is a gauge we can use whenever we have opened up to such a bout and willingly endured it.

Another way of looking at this 'transformation' is that if the arising energy exceeds my bearing tolerance, it will explode, discharge itself. Then with 'all passion spent', I am exhausted and I have to wait until I am 'normal', i.e. charged up again.

But if the energy is not repressed but willingly accepted and contained, when it has burnt itself out, the body feels lighter. Why should that be so? Energy discharged, whether getting tired by physical work or by emotional outbursts, makes me tired and exhausted. If not discharged but contained in the form, i.e. in the body, it gets transformed. It then makes the body feel lighter because there is no more stress. And from that slowly comes the vitality and the willingness to take part in the playing of the great play which life actually is, and with that arises the warmth of the human heart, to be of benefit and use to all.

'The Dharma teachings are manifold, I vow to learn them all.' The Buddha is said to have taught as befitted his audience, sometimes this way and sometimes in another way, using metaphors and parables appropriate to a particular assembly. His Dharma teachings fill libraries and range from the most simple to the most elaborate and profound. But however manifold, all come back to but a few fundamentals. For some people, they were expounded in a roundabout way, and for some it was said straight. To help people of different dispositions we need to learn all the Dharma teachings. And in all the Dharma teachings, there will be one particular version that specifically speaks to me, and along that I can grow until the whole is seen.

It is like seeing one leaf on a twig of a tree. If we follow that one leaf along to the twiglet, the branchlet, the branch, the big branch into the trunk, into the root, we have got the connection. But we have only that one line and we do not as yet know that there are other leaves and other branches or anything else around. And so for the wholeness of it, once we have found our one way to the end, then it is a return up the trunk into the other branches and leaves until the whole, mighty tree is seen. 'The Dharma teachings are manifold, I vow to learn them all.' Then it is possible to realize that there is the way that goes right down from the individual leaf to the root from where it stems and all the others too. Whether great or small, all are nourished by the sap that comes from the root.

A monk grew gourds in a little vegetable patch behind his temple. One morning he heard a frightful din and ran out. There were the gourds shouting at each other. 'No, I am the longest', 'I am the greenest', 'I am the best', 'I am the ripest'. He admonished them, 'Now just stop quarrelling. Look where your stem comes from.' They did so and found that they all came from one root. And that was the end of their quarrel.

'The Buddha Way is supreme, I vow to go it to the end.' It is supreme not because it is the best but because it leads all the way back to where we really come from, to that root which is the end of all strife and of all suffering, as the Buddha proclaimed.

The Dharma teachings are manifold. Only the Buddha could sum them up in just one sentence – 'Suffering I teach and the Way out of suffering.' The suffering comes from the separateness and aloneness that arises from the delusion of a separate I. So we need to go the Way to the end of the separation, to awaken, not only for our own sakes but for all fellow companions on the Way, whether they are consciously on the Buddhist Way or not. If we ourselves have found peace in the heart, the natural warmth in the heart will shine out of itself. In our world, there is so much isolation, so much fear and strife, so much aggression and a deep spiritual hunger. In the office or at home, one person with a warm heart and understanding lightens the situation even if without words.

With this we chant again 'I vow to benefit them all.' I do not need to go out to convert the Papuans in New Guinea or something like that. It is good enough right where I am. Our family, our colleagues at work, that is where we start. Like charity, compassion begins at home. So we also have compassion for ourselves. But there is a great difference between compassion and indulgence. Compassion spreads like ripples in the pond, touching what comes into contact with it.

Number Ten of the Bull-Herding Pictures shows a big, beaming person. It is not because he has suddenly and miraculously grown three times as large as a human being, but he is perceived to be 'large' because he is no longer shrunk into the little I that always looks round to see whether 'I' am still there, whether you approve of me or not and that always feels itself to be hub and centre. And thus it grows ever narrower and smaller and more rigid. Now all this is gone. There is not only warmth but also real understanding and joyfully being of service, for all. That is why we vow to go the Buddha Way to the end.

THE PRACTICE OF CHANTING

In Zen communities, the day is punctuated by chanting. The full chanting is performed first thing in the morning, and the Heart Sutra is chanted at meals while the food is being served. Chanting also precedes the Master's teisho and follows the evening sitting at the end of the day.

As Master Daiyu reminds us in her commentary on the Heart Sutra, the purpose of chanting is to empty the heart. The empty heart (mushin in Japanese) is clear and transparent. Whatever falls into it is seen directly just as it is and can be responded to freely; in the empty heart there is no 'clinging to' or 'rejection of', because there is no I to cling or reject. The Zen chants in this book are presented in the order in which they are chanted morning and evening, and they are a most effective practice for this emptying out. When the chanting is over, at least for a time the mental chatter is quieted, and the inner restlessness that bubbles away at a more subtle level is stilled. One feels at home in the silence.

But experience has shown that there is another very important aspect to the chanting. For us Westerners, the chanting turns out to be an excellent training device, and this is because we tend to have quite a bit of difficulty with it. But if we have patience and perseverance and a willingness to engage with these difficulties, the chanting can teach us almost everything we need to know about wholeheartedness, *samadhi*, (at-oneness) and even no-I.

So how do we chant? When we chant in the meditation hall, we sit on our chairs or kneel on our cushions with our knees together, but otherwise we keep the same good form as we do in meditation. For the first two chants, and for the Four Vows, the hands are held in gassho, which is more or less like the praying position. Those who need the words are allowed to hold a sutra book or sutra sheet in their hands. But it is a good idea to dispense with that as soon as possible and learn the chants off by heart. It is much easier to chant along with the ears than with the eyes. Fortunately, we don't have to know a chant perfectly in order to chant without a prompt. Provided we have made some efforts to learn the words, if we forget what's coming next, or get lost, we can just drop our voice for a moment, and the chanting around us quickly reminds us where to pick up again.

Chanting is a communal activity, and the best way to learn is in a group. If we only ever chant by ourselves, we can develop idiosyncrasies that are hard to eradicate, like the musician who practises alone in his room, only to find he can't play in a band because he now knows how it is done, or thinks he does, and is incapable of listening and responding to what the other band members are actually doing. Zubin Mehta, the Musical Director of the Israel Philharmonic orchestra, and a great conductor of opera, once said, '*Unless you can conduct opera, you cannot call yourself a conductor.*' He explained that in opera, nothing is absolutely fixed. For example, one night the singer might hold on to an important note a little longer, and on another he might change the tempo of a certain passage. The conductor's job is to respond instantly to what the singer is doing and communicate that to the orchestra, without imposing his own idea of what the singer 'ought' to be doing. That of course requires listening, being aware and open, rather than being wrapped in my own personal bubble.

Learning to harmonize with a group is one of the things we Westerners seem to find difficult, and it shows itself by sticking like grim death to the timing and rhythm I have cultivated by myself, or which I think is right. Even some of us who have chanted regularly with the Zen group for years can still be spectacularly inflexible in their chanting, and unable to string together more than three or four syllables with the correct emphasis, even when shown individually. On the other hand – and perhaps not surprisingly – it has been found that musicians are most adept at learning to follow along precisely and accurately, even though they may be quite new to the chanting. One young woman at a weekend retreat stood out for blending in perfectly – if that makes sense – giving each syllable exactly the right length and right stress, and it turned out she was an accomplished amateur flautist. Master Daiyu was once asked, "Do the Japanese have so much difficulty with the chanting as we do?" "No," she replied, "but then they *want* to conform."

"But, yes, yes," we say, "I do want to conform, I really do." And this brings up another problem. As long as I try, I only make things worse, and the harder I try, the worse it gets. For example, I might have an idea of what the chanting should sound like, and I try to produce that sound. Even if I do manage to reproduce it, it always comes out sounding artificial, which of course it is. If I have no one to correct me, I persist in this rut and might even develop some pride in my chanting powers.

But perhaps I will have the good fortune to be corrected. So, I try another voice, perhaps mimicking something I heard on the internet. This time a pinched sound comes out of my nose. And when it finally dawns on me that no amount of trying works, I resolve not to try. But that very resolution is trying as well.

Eventually all I have to show for my efforts is a strangled croak.

To chant naturally means throwing all this I-trying away and diving right into it. Any hesitancy, any thought about getting it right, any self-consciousness gets in the way and blocks the joyous flow. It is no use copying others. Each of us has a different body, a different lung capacity, and different vocal cords. It is not a case of being a great singer, or even being what I might consider a great chanter. That is only my judgement. Although Master Daiyu was a great music lover, she was not a good singer, and only had a small chanting voice. Yet when she chanted, the sound that emerged was full of warmth and gentleness. It reflected what was in her heart and was very moving to hear. On the other hand, Soko Roshi's chanting voice was strong and powerful. There is no one right way. We have to find our own natural voice, the one appropriate to our own particular body. As Master Rinzai famously taught, *"Just be your ordinary selves. Do not give yourselves airs."*

A useful analogy for the chanting is a mountain stream. Falling down the side of the mountain, the stream water twists, turns and dances continuously in its gulley. It is in constant-motion; never for a moment does it stop or pause. In the same way, the syllables of the chant are meant to follow directly on one another, the beginning of one syllable almost tripping over the end of the last, the whole forming an unbroken thread of ever-shifting sound, that begins with the first syllable and dies into silence with the last.

When Soko Roshi came to England for Master Daiyu's ordination, he brought a small retinue of senior monks with him. When they chanted in the little shrine room at Shobo-an, the whole room was filled with sound. Their whole heartedness was physically visible; a couple of the monks looked like the rockets at Cape Canaveral as the engines begin to fire up, and it seemed they were about to lift off from their cushions. This was more of a mountain torrent than a stream. Yet it was not shouting or "roaring in the congregation", as Master Daiyu used to call it. The form was perfect and contained, and they clearly enjoyed chanting together enormously. This brings us to another point.

Chanting is a joyful activity. But it is sometimes difficult to remember that. On the third day of a retreat, for example, we may wake up feeling tired and aching from the long hours of sitting meditation. We take up our seats in the meditation hall dreading the day ahead and wondering why we ever signed up to attend in the first place. And this mood is reflected in the chanting. We feel sorry for ourselves, and chant lifelessly. At these times, Master Daiyu would make us laugh by saying we sounded like the condemned prisoners in the tumbrils, the carts used to convey aristocrats to the guillotine during the French Revolution. Another trap is falling into a marching song, when each syllable is punched out exactly the same: KAN! JI! ZAI! BO! SA! GYO! JIN! HAN! YA! HA! RA! MI! TA! But what we are chanting is, "The Bodhisattva (bo sa) Kanji-zai, deeply coursing in the Wisdom (Prajna) Gone Beyond (Paramita) ..." This leads to a slightly different emphasis, something like Kanji-zai Bosa Gyo Jin Hanya-haramita, with the underlined syllables a little longer. These subtle rhythms make the sutra flow. The particulars differ from school to school and even from temple to temple, but what is important is that the chanting is alive, and to avoid falling into that stiff martial rhythm. Experience has shown that it is quite useless to explain "how to chant"; it is like trying to explain how to ride a bicycle. It can only be learned in the body, by doing it. But there are one or two useful pointers that can be given. First, the chanting is 90 per cent vowels, and the consonants are quite soft. If the consonants are articulated too strongly, the flow is interrupted by the lips opening and closing, and the stream of sound keeps stopping and starting. So we aim for a constant carrier wave or stream that is modulated by the syllables of the chant, and it is only necessary to move the lips slightly. In this way, the carrier wave keeps going steadily regardless of the syllables and can be heard as an underlying forward motion driving the chant on. It only breaks when we need to draw breath. In a group everyone runs out of breath at different times, so the overall sound never stops.

When we have got used to the chanting, and can chant whole-heartedly and joyfully, pressing on without a break, there comes a switching point where the fundamental character of the chanting changes. The sound now seems to pour out effortlessly, all by itself. A pleasurable sensation fills the body and lifts us up. There is chanting, but no chanter. Harmonising is no problem either. Everything is heard clearly; and if the group speeds up or changes the rhythm, the response is instant and automatic, and all that might be necessary is to apply the brakes now and then, to prevent me going to the other extreme and being carried away. Even this is not necessary after I have got used to it. This going-by-itself is the *samadhi* of chanting.

But even when we experience the chanting like this, it still needs be cultivated. If we are not careful, we can easily fall back into in a state of faux *samadhi* or automatic pilot, where I am chanting quite acceptably, but my mind is somewhere else, caught up in one of my favourite thought trains. This tells us we are by no means done with the chanting practice. I am still there and have only managed to get out of the way temporarily. The remedy can be found in the Buddha's foundational teaching of the Noble Eightfold Path.

The Noble Eightfold Path is divided into three sections, and the section known as *samadhi* consists of three factors: (1) effort, best thought of here as the effort of giving ourselves into the chanting; (2) *sati* (awareness, best thought of here as recollection) and (3) *samadhi* itself. When we get caught in a thought train, sati is lost and we no longer know where we are or what is being done; effort is needed to recollect ourselves once more, and once again dissolve into the chant, so there is nothing of I left in the heart. Continuously cultivating the chanting in this way is therefore in accord with the Noble Eightfold Path. It is also an excellent way of learning how to empty the heart so it can function, unobstructed by I, in accordance with what is.

Garry Gelade, London 2019

THE DAILY CHANTS OF
THE ZEN CENTRE, LONDON

May this chanting and sitting benefit all sentient beings.
May all beings attain Buddhahood.

The Daily Chants of the Zen Centre, London were copied from
the Hampshire Buddhist Society's Booklet, *Daily Chanting*.

ZANGE MON
Ga sha-ku sho-zo sho aku-go kai-yu mu-shi to jin chi ju
shin ku i shi sho-sho is-sai ga kon kai zan-ge.

Repentance
All the evil Karma created by me from of old out of beginningless greed, anger and delusion, committed with body speech
and thought, of all this I now make full and open repentance.

SAN KI-KAI
Na-mu kie butsu na-mu kie ho na-mu kie so kie butsu mujo
son kie ho ri-yoku son kie so wa-go son kie buk-kyo kie ho-kyo
kie so-kyo nyo-rai shi-shin to-shogaku ze ga daishi ga kon kie
ju-kon yo sho-butsu i-shi ko fu-kie ja-ma ge-do ji-min-ko ji-min-
ko dai-ji-min-ko.

The Three Refuges
I take refuge in the Buddha, I take refuge in the Dharma, I
take refuge in the Sangha. I take refuge in the Buddha, the
most venerable one. I take refuge in the Dharma, venerable in

its purity. I take refuge in the Sangha, venerable in its harmony. I have taken refuge in the Buddha, I have taken refuge in the Dharma, I have taken refuge in the Sangha. In the true Tathagata of complete and perfect enlightenment I put my faith, he is my great Master; I will rely on him as my teacher and not follow evil demons or other ways. Out of compassion, out of compassion, out of great compassion.

MA-KA HAN-NYA HA-RA-MI-TA SHIN-GYO

Kan-ji-zai bo-sa gyo jin han-nya ha-ra-mi-ta ji sho-ken go-un kai ku do is-sai ku-yaku sha-ri-shi shiki fu-i ku ku fu-i shiki shiki soku ze ku ku soku ze shiki ju so gyo shiki yaku bu nyo ze sha-ri-shi ze sho-ho ku-so fu-sho fu-metsu fu-ku fu-jo fu-zo fu-gen ze ko ku-chu mu-shiki mu ju so gyo shiki mu gen ni bi zes-shin-i mu shiki sho ko mi soku ho mu-gen-kai nai-shi mu-i-shiki-kai mu-mumyo yaku mu-mu-myo-jin nai-shi mu-ro-shi yaku mu-ro shi-jin mu ku shu metsu do mu chi yaku mu toku i musho tok-ko bo-dai-sat-ta e han-nya ha-ra-mi-ta ko shin mu-kei-ge mu-kei-ge ko mu u ku fu on-ri is-sai ten-do mu-so ku-gyo ne-han san-ze sho-butsu e han-nya ha-rami- ta ko toku a-noku-ta-ra sam-myaku sam-bo-dai ko chi han-nya ha-ra-mi-ta ze dai-jin-shu ze dai-myo-shu ze mujo- shu ze mu-to-do-shu no jo is-sai ku shin-jitsu fu-ko ko setsu han-nya ha-ra-mi-ta shu soku setsu shu watsu gya-tei gya-tei hara-gya-tei hara-so-gya-tei bo ji so-wa-ka han-nya shingyo.

The Heart of the Great Wisdom Sutra

When the Bodhisattva Avalokitesvara practised the profound Great Wisdom Gone Beyond (*prajña paramita*) he clearly saw that the Five Aggregates (*skandha)* are all empty and thus passed

beyond suffering. Oh Sariputra, form is not different from emptiness, emptiness is not different from form. Form is emptiness,
emptiness is form. The same applies also to feeling or sensation, perception, mental configurations and consciousness.
Oh Sariputra, all things (*dharmas*) are in themselves empty,
neither coming to be nor ceasing to be, neither pure nor impure,
neither increasing nor decreasing. Thus within emptiness there
is no form, no feeling or sensation, no perception, no mental
configurations, no consciousness. Within emptiness there is no
eye, no ear, no nose, no tongue, no body, no mind; there is no
field of seeing, of hearing, of smelling, of tasting, of touching,
no field of consciousness. Within emptiness there is no delusion
nor extinction of delusion and so on (through the twelve links
of the Chain of Dependent Causation) to old age and death, nor
extinction of old age and death. Within emptiness there is no
suffering, no cause of suffering, no end of suffering, and no way
to the end of suffering. Within emptiness there is no knowledge,
nor any attainment either, and nothing that can be attained.
The Bodhisattva relies on the Great Wisdom Gone Beyond and
so his heart is free of hindrances. Because his heart is free
of hindrances, he is free of fear. Going beyond all error and
delusion, he enters final Nirvana. All past, present and future
Buddhas rely on the Great Wisdom Gone Beyond and so attain
to Perfect and Complete Awakening. Know therefore that the
Great Wisdom Gone Beyond is the Great Mantra, the Wisdom
Mantra which is supreme and peerless, and delivers from all suf-
fering. It is true, not vain; therefore I proclaim the Mantra of the
Great Wisdom Gone Beyond and I proclaim it thus: GATE GATE
PARAGATE PARASAMGATE BODHl SVAHA! (Gone, Gone, Gone
Beyond, Gone altogether Beyond, Enlightenment Fulfilled.)

SHO-SAI-SHU

Na-mu sa-man-da mo-to-nan o-ha-ra-chi ko-to-sha so-nonan
to-ji-to en gya-gya gya-ki gya-ki un-nun shi-fu-ra shifu- ra ha-ra-
shi-fu-ra ha-ra-shi-fu-ra chi-shu-sa chi-shu-sa shu-shi-ri shu-shi-ri
so-ha-ja so-ha-ja se-chi-gya shi-ri-ei so-mo-ko.

Dharani of Removing Disasters
Adoration to all the Buddhas!
Adoration to the Teaching that knows no obstructions!
Thus: .... (speak, speak)!
.... (blaze, blaze)!
.... (burst, burst)!
One who is quiescent!
To the glorious one, hail!

DAI-HI-SHU

Na-mu ka-ra-tan-no to-ra-ya-ya na-mu o-ri-ya bo-ryo-kichi shi-fu-
ra-ya fu-ji-sa-to-bo-ya mo-ko-sa-to-bo-ya moko kya-ru-ni-kya-ya
yen sa ha-ra ha-ei shu-ta-no ton-sha na-mu shi-ki-ri to i-mo o-ri-ya
bo-ryo-ki-chi shi-fu-ra ri-to bo na-mu no-ra ki-ji ki-ri mo-ko-ho-
do sha-mi sa-bo o to cho shu-ben o-shu-in sa-bo sa-to no-mo-bo
gya mo-ha te-cho to ji to en o-bo-ryo-ki ryo-gya-ch i-kya-ra-chi
yu-kiri mo-ko fu-ji-sa-to sa-bo sa-bo mo-ra mo-ra mo-ki mo-ki
ri-to-in ku-ryo ku-ryo ke-mo to-ryo to-ryo ho-ja ya-chi mo-ko
ho-ja ya-chi to-ra to-ra chi-ri-ni shi-fu-ra-ya sha-ro sha-ro mo-mo
ha-mo-ra ho-chi-ri yu-ki yu-ki shi-no shino o-ra san fu-ra-sha-ri
ha-ja ha-ja fu-ra-sha-ya ku-ryo ku-ryo mo-ra ku-ryo ku-ryo ki-ri
sha-ro sha-ro shi-ri shi-ri su-ryo su-ryo fu-ji-ya fu-ji-ya fu-do-ya
fu-do-ya mi-chi-riya no-ra kin-ji chi-ri-shu-ni-no ho-ya-mo-no
so-mo-ko shi-do-ya so-mo-ko mo-ko shi-do-ya so-mo-ko shi-do

yu-ki shi-fu-ra-ya so-mo-ko no-ra kin-ji so-mo-ko mo-ra no-ra
so-mo-ko shi-ra sun-o mo-gya-ya so-mo-ko so-bo mo-ko shi-
do-ya so-mo-ko sha-ki-ra o-shi-do-ya so-moko ho-do-mo-gya
shi-do-ya so-mo-ko no-ra kin-ji ha-gyara-ya so-mo-ko mo-ho-ri
shin-gya-ra-ya so-mo-ko na-mu ka-ra-tan-no to-ra-ya-ya na-mu
o-ri-ya bo-ryo-ki-chi shi-fu-ra-ya so-mo-ko shi-te-do mo-do-ra
ho-do-ya so-mo-ko.

Dharani of the Great Compassionate One
Adoration to the Triple Treasure! Adoration to Avalokitesvara,
the Bodhisattva-Mahasattva who is the great compassionate one!
Om, to the one who performs a leap beyond all fears! Having
adored him may I enter into the heart of the blue-necked one
known as the noble adorable Avalokitesvara! It means the com-
pleting of all meaning, it is pure, it is that which makes all beings
victorious and cleanses the path of existence. Thus: Om, the
seer, the worldtranscending one! O Hari, the Mahabodhisattva!
All, all. Defilement, defilement! The earth, the earth! It is the
heart. Do, do the work! Hold fast, hold fast! O great victor! Hold
on, hold on! I hold on. To Indra the creator! Move, move my
defilement-free seal! Come, come! Hear, hear! A joy springs up
in me! Speak, speak! Directing! Hulu, hulu, mala, hulu, hulu,
hile! Sara, sara! Siri, siri! Suru, suru! Be awakened, be awakened!
Have awakened, have awakened! O merciful one, blue-necked
one! Of daring ones, to the joyous, hail! To the boar-faced one,
hail! To the one with a lion's head and face, hail! To the one
who holds a sword in his hand, hail! To the one who holds a
wheel in his hand, three hail! To the one who holds a lotus in
his hand, hail! To the blue-necked far-causing one, hail! To
the beneficent one referred to in this Dharani beginning with

'Nama', hail! Adoration to the Triple treasure! Adoration to Avalokitesvara! Hail! May these (prayers) be successful! To this magical formula, hail!

TEI DAI DEN PO BU SO NO MYO GO

Bibashi Butsu Shiki Butsu Bishafu Butsu Kuruson Butsu Kunagonmuni Butsu Kasho Butsu Shakamuni Butsu Makkakasho Sonja Anan Sonja Shonawashu Sonja Ubakikuta Sonja Daitaka Sonja Mishaka Sonja Bashumitsu Sonja Buddanandai Sonja Fukudamitta Sonja Kyo Sonja Funayasha Sonja Memyo Sonja Kabimora Sonja Ryuju Sonja Kanadaiba Sonja Ragorata Sonja Sogyanandai Sonja Kayashata Sonja Kumorata Sonja Shayata Sonja Bashubanzu Sonja Manura Sonja Kakurokuna Sonja Shishi Sonja Bashashita Sonja Funyomitta Sonja Hannyatara Sonja Bodaidaruma Daishi Eka Daiso Zenji Sosan Kanchi Zenji Doshin Daii Zenji Gunin Daiman Zenji Eno Daikan Zenji Nangaku Ejo Zenji Baso Doitsu Zenji Hyakujo Ekai Zenji Obaku Kiun Zenji Rinzai Gigen Zenji Koke Zonsho Zenji Nanin Egyo Zenji Fuketsu Ensho Zenji Shuzan Shonen Zenji Funyo Zensho Zenji Sekiso Soen Zenji Yogi Hoe Zenji Hakuun Shutan Zenji Goso Hoen Zenji Engo Kokugon Zenji Kukyu Joryu Zenji Oan Donge Zenji Mittan Kanketsu Zenji Shogen Sugaku Zenji Unnan Fugan Zenji Kido Chigu Zenji Nanpo Jomyo Zenji Shuho Myocho Zenji Kanzan Egen Zenji Juo Sohitsu Zenji Muin Soin Zenji Nippo Soshun Zenji Giten Gensho Zenji Sekko Soshin Zenji Toyo Eicho Zenji Taiga Tankyo Zenji Koho Genkun Zenji Sensho Zuisho Zenji lan Chisatsu Zenji Tosen Soshin Zenji Yozan Keiyo Zenji Gudo Toshoku Zenji Shido Bunan- Zenji Dokyo Etan Zenji Hakuin Ekaku Zenji Gassan Jito Zenji Inzan len Zenji Taigan Shigen Zenji Gisan Zenrai Zenji Kosen Soon Zenji

Kogaku Soen Zenji Tetsuo Sokatsu Zenji Zuigan Soseki Zenji
Sesso Soho Zenji Daiyu Myokyo Zenji

The Line of Transmission
As this consists of names only, there is no need for any transla-
tion. It starts with the traditional seven Buddhas, Sakyamuni
Buddha being the seventh. He is followed by Kasyapa, Ananda,
and so on, including Nagarjuna (Ryuju Sonja) to Bodhidharma
Daishi, the twenty-eighth Indian and first Chinese patriarch.
From there on the title 'Sonja' of the Indian patriarchs changes
to 'Zenji'. Kido Chigu Zenji is the last Chinese patriarch in
the Japanese tradition of the Daitoku-ji and Myoshin-ji line of
Rinzai Zen, with Nanpo Jomyo Zenji and Shuho Myocho Zenji
(Daio and Daito Kokushi respectively) as the first and second
Japanese patriarchs.

KOZEN DALTO KOKUSHL YULKAL
Nanjira shonin kono sanchu ni kitatte dono tame ni kobe o
atsumu ejiki no tame ni suru koto nakare kata atte kizu to yu
koto naku kuchi atte kurawazu to yu koto nashi tada subekaraku
junijichu murie no tokoro ni mukatte kiwame kitari kiwame
saru beshi koin ya no gotoshi tsutsushinde zoyoshin suru koto
nakare. Kanshu seyo kanshu seyo!

Roso angya no nochi aruiwa jimon hanko bukkaku kyokan
kin gin o chiribame tashu nyonetsu aruiwa jukyo fuju choza
fuga ichijiki bosai rokuji gyodo tatoi immo ni shi saru to iedomo
busso fuden no myodo o motte kyokan ni kazai sezunba tachi-
machi inga o hatsumu shi shinpu chi ni otsu mina kore jama
no shuzoku nari. Roso yo o saru koto hisashiku tomo jison to
shozuru koto o yurasaji aruiwa ichinin ari yagai ni menzetsu

shi ippa botei sekkyakusho nai ni yasaikon o nite kisshite hi o sugosu tomo sen'itsu ni koji o kyumei suru tei wa roso to nichinichi shoken ho ontei no hito nari. Tare ka aete kyokotsu sen ya. Bensen! Bensen!

National Teacher Daito on his Deathbed Admonished His Monks:

'All you monks who come to this mountain monastery, remember why you are assembled here: you have gathered for the practice of the Way, and not for food and clothing. While you have shoulders, you have clothes to wear, and while you have mouths, you have food to eat. Throughout the twelve periods of the day, devote yourselves unceasingly to the perception of the Inconceivable. Time flies like an arrow; be reverent, do not allow your hearts to chase after the manifold. Take heed, take heed!

After my pilgrimage (death) you might be incumbents of richly endowed temples, towers and halls with Sutra books all inlaid with gold and silver, and devotees crowding all around. Or you may read Sutras and chant Dharanis, or sit in meditation for long hours without sleep, eat but one meal a day, while keeping all the religious observances throughout the six periods. Yet unless you truly dwell in your heart on the wonderful Way that cannot be transmitted by Buddha and patriarchs, you will fail to bring forth the fruit and cause the downfall of the true line. Such as these belong to the family of evil spirits and may not call themselves my descendants, no matter how long ago I have departed from this world. But if there is just one person, although living in a remote wilderness in a hut thatched with just one bundle of reeds and eating wild plants and roots cooked in a pot with broken legs, yet if he but wholeheartedly applies himself to investigating and clarifying the One Great Matter, he

sees me face to face every day and requites his debt of gratitude.
Who would dare to despise such a one? Be diligent, be diligent!'

SHI-GU SEI-GAN
Shu-jo mu-hen sei-gan-do bon-no mu-jin sei-gan-dan
homon mu-ryo sei-gan-gaku butsu-do mu-jo sei-gan-jo.

The Four Great Vows
Sentient beings are numberless, I vow to benefit them all.
The afflicting passions are inexhaustible, I vow to end them all.
The Dharma teachings are manifold, I vow to learn them all.
The Buddha Way is supreme, I vow to go it to the end.